Sandra Scarr and Judy Dunn

Mother Care/Other Care

Penguin Books

Penguin Books Ltd, Harmondsworth, Middlesex, England
Viking Penguin Inc., 40 West 23rd Street, New York, New York 10010, U.S.A.
Penguin Books Australia Ltd, Ringwood, Victoria, Australia
Penguin Books Canada Limited, 2801 John Street, Markham, Ontario, Canada L3R 1B4
Penguin Books (N.Z.) Ltd, 182–190 Wairau Road, Auckland 10, New Zealand

First published in the U.S.A. by Basic Books, New York, 1984
Second edition published in Great Britain in Pelican Books 1987

Made and printed in Great Britain by
Cox & Wyman Ltd, Reading
Filmset in Linotron Aldus by
Rowland Phototypesetting Ltd, Bury St Edmunds, Suffolk

PELICAN BOOKS

Mother Care/Other Care

Sandra Scarr is Commonwealth Professor of Psychology at the University of Virginia. Prior to this she spent six years as Professor of Psychology at Yale University and before that, six years as Professor of Child Psychology at the University of Minnesota. Her research on such topics as child development, intelligence, education and behaviour has been published in over one hundred articles and books. A Fellow of the American Psychological Association and the American Association for the Advancement of Science, she has also been elected by her colleagues to many professional posts including the Presidency of the Division on Developmental Psychology of the American Psychological Association.

Sandra Scarr has served on the editorial boards of several psychology journals and as the Editor of the APA journal *Developmental Psychology*. She lives with her husband, four children, two dogs and two cats and her interests include gardening and American football.

Judy Dunn studied at Cambridge and became a developmental psychologist. She is now a Fellow of King's College, Cambridge, and carries out her research for the Medical Research Council at Cambridge. Her special interests lie in the development of young children and their family relationships, and in the lives of mothers with young children. She has conducted several longitudinal studies of children in Britain, pioneered research on sibling relationships in early childhood, and collaborated on a major study of adopted children and their siblings in the United States. She is the author of a number of books including *Distress and Comfort* (1977), *Siblings: Love, Envy and Understanding* (1982), *Sisters and Brothers* (1984), *The First Year of Life* (1979, with David Shaffer) and *The Study of Temperament* (1986, with Robert Plomin). Judy Dunn has three children, a daughter and twin sons.

Contents

Preface

This book has both personal and professional roots. It is about a concern – common to both of us though we live and work in cultures that are in many respects different – with the lives of women and children in Britain today, and with the question of how beliefs about the development of children affect those lives. Exclusive mothering (as opposed to fathering and care by others) is stressed in Britain today – stressed as crucial for the well-being of our children. But what kinds of care do babies *really* need in order to thrive? What are the consequences of other kinds of care? For financial reasons, many women cannot provide this exclusive mothering. They have to work. And many other women *want* to be involved in employment outside the home. Are they subjecting their children to stressful or damaging experiences? How can they judge the quality of care other than their own? One focus of the book is this: the question of how parents can best meet the needs of their children at different ages and stages.

A second focus is the question of *why* there is the emphasis today on exclusive mothering. Other societies, and our own culture at other times, have not stressed the exclusive importance of mothers for their children's normal development. The question led us to trace the development of current ideas about mothers' roles and children's needs – the changing image of motherhood in Britain. A glimpse of how that image has altered with social, economic and political changes in our world should alert us to be sceptical of dogmatic pronouncements on the crucial importance of exclusive mothering.

Yet mothers faced with making decisions about their family and their work frequently hear only the dogmatic pronouncements on the dire consequences of a decision to work. Our hope in writing this book is that information about mothers, children and child care will help those young parents today who are faced with making such decisions. Mothers have a right to know what is known about the consequences of different kinds of care for children, and psychologists have a responsibility to tell them. There *are* solutions to the seeming incompatibility of careers and family life. And there are social changes that need to be made to accommodate the realities of life for working parents in the 1980s. The larger society promotes categorical views about what is right and good for families without regard for the realities of many parents' and children's lives. This book, based on recent research and extensive professional and personal experience with child care and the problems and dilemmas faced by mothers, is intended to help to right the balance.

The personal and professional roots of the book are our own experiences as researchers in developmental psychology, as women working in a man's world of university teachers, and as mothers facing the practicalities and worries of combining family and work lives. The genesis of the book lay in Sandra Scarr's plans to write a scholarly monograph on child care outside the home, based on research – her own and others' – on the effects of high- and low-quality care on babies and young children. The more she thought about research on child care, however, the more she wanted to broaden the message to a book about child care as it affects the lives of women and children. A volume *Mother Care/Other Care*, published by Basic Books in the United States in 1984, was the result.

This book takes the same themes, and examines them in the context of Britain. The history of attitudes towards working mothers, and of social policies towards mothers and children, differs between the two countries, as do the choices (or lack of them) about provision that mothers face. Our own decisions about the full-time-mother-or-professional-person dilemma also differed, as did our professional backgrounds and our experiences as working mothers. But the commonalities are striking too: commonalities in what we regard as central themes in developmental psychology that are directly relevant to choices about child care, commonalities in the worries and problems that are faced by mothers in both our cultures. The specific details may differ but the issues are far broader than the policy concerns of a particular country.

One commonality between us and other working mothers in our two countries is that, with no community provision for day care, each of us concocted an individual solution to the social problem of how to care for our children while we worked. And we did little directly to change community attitudes towards working mothers. We merely played the game as men wrote the rules.

Both of us had long thought that we, as professionals-and-mothers in particular, were the harbingers of the future. We now think that we were accomplices in the continuation of a system to deny women and children what they need when women are the mothers of young children. It is our hope that this book will help to change that system.

We want to thank Judith Greissman, of Basic Books, who encouraged Sandra Scarr to write the book on the US, and enthusiastically supported our collaboration on this book. Our thanks to her for all her confidence, help and inspiration. For the research on child care in Britain we have drawn especially on the work of Jack and Barbara Tizard, whose contribution to our understanding of child care in Britain has been immeasurable; on the research of their colleagues at the Thomas Coram Research Unit, London University; and on the findings of the Oxford Pre-school Project which was headed by Jerome Bruner, supported by the SSRC. The research on day care in the US was the product of joyful collaboration between Sandra Scarr, Kathleen McCartney of Harvard University, J. Conrad Schwarz of the University of Connecticut, Deborah Phillips of the University of Illinois, and Susan Grajek of Yale University. That research was supported by the W. T. Grant Foundation, UNESCO, and the Government of Bermuda.

While writing this book, we have been supported by the Center for Advanced Study at the University of Virginia (SS) and the Center for Advanced Study in the Behavioral Sciences, Stanford, the Medical Research Council and the John D. and Catherine T. MacArthur Foundation (JD). We are both deeply grateful for the opportunity given us to think and write.

Finally, this book is dedicated to our own seven children: Stephanie, Rebecca, Karen, Phillip, and Paul, William and Sophie.

PART ONE

Dilemmas of Modern Motherhood

CHAPTER ONE

To Be or Not to Be a Working Mother

Employment outside the home is now a choice, or necessity, for the majority of mothers with pre-school children. How are the babies to be cared for while the mother works? Today a mother must chart the unknowns of child-care arrangements down the rapids of conflicting advice. If she has a choice, should she or shouldn't she work outside the home, leaving the baby to what may be the vagaries of others' care – others who may not have a mother's commitment to the child's development? Will leaving the baby with someone else stifle his emotional growth? Will the baby feel abandoned? Will he ever love again? How can a child become as bright and clever as she could be if her mother is not at home to show her the picture books and baby games that foster her intelligence? Guilt and anxiety haunt every mother who faces such questions. And women often face them alone.

The decision to work or not while children are very young is a personal event, based on many economic, social and psychological factors that affect every family in different ways. This book will not tell you whether or not to work, but it will free you from some common misconceptions about the effects of maternal employment on babies and young children. It is a book about child-care options and their consequences. Happily, children can have good care, whether mothers stay at home or go to work outside the home. Babies thrive on good day care, just as they do at home with a loving and attentive mother. In fact, children are usually better off with a happy part-time mother and satisfied substitute caregivers than with a depressed or frustrated full-time mother.

There are, however, some kinds of child care to be avoided in the best interests of children. Children's needs change as they grow up, so that what constitutes good care for four-year-olds will not meet the needs of toddlers, and vice versa. And there is some care that is not good for anyone. This book will describe what is good and what is poor care, and the research that leads to these conclusions.

Women and Children

This book is also about women and children in Britain today. Our society sends mixed messages about women's rights and women's proper place. Such mixed messages about whether mothers are *supposed* to have jobs are a symptom of larger questions about what women are supposed to be. Closely linked to the politics of what women ought to be is the psychology of what children are supposed to need. In Chapter 3 we will look at the relationship between the position of women and the psychology of childhood as it has evolved in this century.

A major question addressed by this book is why mothers of young children suffer so much uncertainty about what they are *supposed* to do for their small children. Why is the culture so clear on what is right for men to do and so vague on women's decisions that depart even so slightly from tradition? Husbands are *supposed* to work outside the home; they are *not supposed* to stay at home to take care of the children. Mothers, on the other hand, should stay at home *unless* there are compelling reasons to be employed outside the home. The list that follows 'unless' is disturbingly long and complexly weighted.

Most women are understandably confused about how to evaluate the conflicting claims of more income for the family, their own longing to be with their babies, the virtue of mother love for babies, the need to continue their own careers before it's too late, the self-respect that comes from being paid for one's own efforts, the pride of husbands in being able to support their families single-handedly, the harm that might befall the children without a full-time mother, the meals that won't get cooked, the dust under the sofa, and so forth. One solution is to try to do it all.

Ellen Goodman, writing for the *Boston Globe*, sums up the conflicts women face today. Comparing the Supermum of every-woman's imagined past with the ideal Superwoman of today, she says:

Supermom, for those of you who don't remember or don't have one, was the one who always made homemade cookies with carrot teeth and raisin eyes. She always had 'something lovin'' in the oven. Her kids always had homemade Halloween costumes. She had a wide wardrobe, consisting exclusively of aprons. She was always nurturing. For years we have carried her around in our heads, just for the guilt of it. Now we have replaced her with Superwoman or Supermom II, whose typical day is something like the following: She wakes up to her 2.6 children. They go downstairs and she gives them a Grade A nutritional breakfast which they eat, and they all go off to school without once forgetting their lunch money. She goes upstairs to get dressed in her $300 Anne Klein suit and goes off to her $25,000 job which is both creative and socially useful. After work she comes home and spends a wonderful hour relating with the children, because after all it is not the quantity but the quality of time that is important. She then prepares a gourmet dinner for her husband. They spend time working on their meaningful relationship, after which they go upstairs where she has multiple orgasms until midnight (Goodman, 1980, pp. 5–6).

The companion for Supermum II is Superdad, who is always caring, sharing, and able to leap tall emotional barriers in a single bound, while he is also becoming president of the company. Goodman concludes that we all feel guilty because we cannot live up to the old images of apron-clad motherhood, nor can we make it as Superparent. There is simply not enough time or energy to excel at all those tasks. We may pretend to the throne when serving homemade pâté to the dinner guests or coaching toddler soccer, after a full day at the office. We may even pretend to ourselves from time to time, but something is bound to go wrong with so demanding a role.

The last dinner party one of us gave took two days out of her life, days when no writing was done and no child got more than a fleeting hello. Yet we assure you she was smiling graciously over the carefully arranged garden flowers and quiche, as though the whole affair were merely a trifle in her Supermum's life. But we all know that such occasions disrupt work and child-care schedules. Unless one wants to become a full-time caterer, rather than a writer and mother, one does not give many such parties. One needs to ask, 'What's it all about, anyway?'

Mothers' responsibilities are awesome enough. But even if you can juggle the schedule, get to work on time, get children to the dentist, and find good child care that you can afford, you still may not feel comfortable about the decision. The next section deals with a major worry.

For Better or for Worse

Suppose that you have a young child and have decided to work. Like all women before you, you will have to find suitable child care. Many problems of obtaining good child care can be solved with money. But other issues of working and child care trade in a currency of guilt, it seems. Mixed messages about whether or not you should work and what your child's best interests are can affect your mental health more directly than finding child-care arrangements, however difficult that may be. If you are like most working mothers, you face a hostile community of relatives, neighbours and professionals telling you that a mother should stay at home with her baby. Besides, your own feelings of attachment may make it difficult for you to leave your baby. Let us look at the immediate social environment of the working mother: her relatives and the advice-givers – doctors and psychologists appearing on TV and writing in magazines. What advice do these important people give to working mothers?

What will the relatives say?

Attitudes about maternal employment in professional and popular magazines are ambivalent at best. Clair Etaugh (1980) documented a predominantly disapproving attitude toward working mothers in the popular press, the main themes being neglect of the children, neglect of the husband and neglect of homemaking. Unless a mother has to work to keep her family from starvation, many people are suspicious of her motives. Is she so selfish as to seek her own satisfactions at the expense of her babies and her husband? Older women and men are more likely to have negative views about working women than are younger people. Unfortunately, these older people are likely to be our parents, aunts, and uncles. Their disapproval can be painful.

Some professionals, such as Burton L. White (1981), still advise mothers to stay home with their young children, for reasons we will review in Chapter 4. Other professionals, such as Joanne Curry O'Connell (1983), argue in the same journals that such advice is unwarranted, for reasons we will discuss in Chapter 5. Suffice it to say here that there is tremendous ambivalence in the professional and popular press about mothers who work outside the home.

Our own histories are similar, we think, to those of many professional women – although the two of us had rather different experiences combining motherhood and work, and coped in different ways with the choices and tasks that faced us. Sandra Scarr had one child before she finished a Ph.D. in psychology and was eager both to find an academic job and to have more children:

Though I was confident that I could do a good job at both motherhood and career, I found my relatives uniformly arrayed against my working at a career. My subsequent success made no difference in their attitudes. Weekly telephone calls from my mother always contained the question, 'And when are you going to quit work and take proper care of your child(ren)?' She unfailingly sent newspaper and magazine clippings about the dangers of maternal employment to children's mental health, with admonitions that I should be certain to read them and discuss them with my children's doctor. I gathered she was confident that he would set me straight about my responsibilities.

At family gatherings I could count on several of the college-educated cousins, full-time homemakers, chiding me on leaving my poor baby (babies) with a housekeeper or day-care home. Their being at home full time was so much better for their children, they assured me. Never mind the fact that they often left the children with babysitters while they played bridge, volunteered on neighbourhood committees, shopped, and took courses on flower-arranging. The fact that I was employed made the whole child-rearing scene different in their view. I will never forget one reunion when I proudly announced my new position as a tenured Associate Professor at the University of Pennsylvania. The relatives moaned that my (then) two children would suffer for my success.

In 1969 I wrote a letter to *Science*, the prestigious journal of the American Association for the Advancement of Science, to protest the unfair treatment of women in universities, who were expected to work full time like men and be fully responsible for their children's welfare.

> Once a female professor has decided to demonstrate her dedication by male rules, the larger community which judges her children's well-being may undermine her in capricious ways. Schools schedule mothers' meetings during teaching hours; the guidance counsellor decides that a child with a fully employed mother needs 'special' attention; ordinary school and neighborhood 'scrapes' that her children experience are attributed to mother's neglect. The professional mother is vulnerable because in the eyes of many she is not doing the best for her children (1969, p. 1260).

But that was the 1960s and 1970s – Dark Ages for Maternal Employment. The culture has surely become more tolerant, or has it? A former student of mine, now an Assistant Professor at Harvard, says that her mother asks her the same question: 'When *are* you going to quit work and take care of your baby?' Other relatives ask her how *does* she manage, with shakes of the head and implicit disapproval. So much for progress in relatives' attitudes towards working mothers.

Judy Dunn had three babies within eighteen months while still a student and gave up plans for working for several years, chiefly because of a concern for what the consequences might be for the children:

> My concern about what it would mean for the children if I worked more than very part time overwhelmed any plans to carry on a serious career. It meant that when I did start work I only worked part time for a long while, and took a long time to feel confident in my job, even with a very supportive husband. I *loved* being at home with the children, but it was without question more difficult (I now know needlessly difficult) to begin a professional life after the break.

Relations with one's sisters, cousins, and friends who stay home with their babies while you work can also pose problems. Despite claims of tolerance on both sides, unemployed mothers often envy working women and need to justify their decision to stay at home by questioning the adequacy of day-care arrangements. Employed mothers often envy mothers at home for the time they have with their children and anxiously compare their own children's progress with that of babies with full-time mothers. In the 1980s we have not resolved the costs and benefits of maternal employment to anyone's real satisfaction. We think that the lack of resolution results more from conflicting cultural values about women and children than from any demonstrated good or bad effects of mothers' working or staying at home.

The major problem of relatives' and friends' disapproval of your working is that you know you will be blamed for anything that goes wrong with your child. If he has problems of any kind – social, emotional, intellectual or physical – you will be responsible for not having provided a proper home. Everything from shyness to ingrowing toenails can be attributed to your working, not to mention major mental illnesses and mental retardation. If she does well, she will have succeeded *despite* your neglect. If your child turns out to be a star, don't count on accolades for a job well done.

The lament is not applicable to professional women only. Any employed mother is a target for traditional blame, should anything be amiss with her children. Even the ordinary, everyday problems of children growing up become ammunition against her for being employed.

The Guilt Trip; How Will Your Working Affect the Children?

Give a woman the smallest latitude to deviate from her ordinary role, and the experts hover around her with dire warnings about the consequences of her contemplated action for those she loves. So far, the culture has kept women in a limbo of ambiguity about their roles as mothers. Experts who control information about what is good for children have been no more sympathetic to the dilemmas of personhood and motherhood than the ordinary person on the street. Now, however, there is more research on questions about child care that does not start with the assumption that a mother should stay at home full time with her child.

There is an element of irony in the special relationship that today's culture demands of women and children. How did children come to be the special responsibility of their mothers, rather than of their fathers or the larger society? Although the answer to this question may seem obvious to people brought up in the twentieth century, mothers have not always had the most important role in their children's upbringing, when they had other economic roles to play. At some points in the past, fathers were the key parent in the upbringing of the next generation, because moral training, not emotional sensitivity, was thought to be central to successful child rearing. Mothers were thought to corrupt their little ones with too much affection and not enough stern training.

Today, guilt is inflicted on mothers who consider working and leaving their babies in others' care. Not only do friends and relatives suggest in subtle and not so subtle ways that we neglect our children if we choose to work after motherhood, but we have built-in sources of guilt that give each of us nightmares. Are we damaging, neglecting or depriving our children by leaving them in order to work?

Expert advice

Most mothers fear that putting their babies in day care will ruin them or their own relationship with them. These fears did not spring spontaneously into each of our heads, independently. Such fears are promoted by child-development experts who advise mothers to stay at home with their young children lest the children be warped for life. Of course, the experts are far from unanimous on this point. Psychologists, psychiatrists, paediatricians and other parents all give advice, much of it conflicting and all of it dependent on beliefs of the larger culture, as we discuss in Chapters 2, 3 and 4.

From a cacophony of conflicting advice, parents are supposed to sort out what is important for their babies and pre-school children and to act accordingly. Not only is their own behaviour in question, but the substitute care they provide for their infants and young children is suspected to be the child's potential ruination. Rearing a child according to the advice of some experts can be hazardous to your mental health. It is comforting to know that expert advice has changed dramatically in this century. Much current advice is out of step with the times and with recent research on maternal employment and child care.

In the 1920s, prevailing expert advice was to curb children, who were viewed as impulsive little creatures in need of stern training. Children's nurturance could not safely be left in the hands of sentimental parents, whose undisciplined affection could thwart the stern habit-training of the day. The 1950s view was of fragile flowers, who thrive only in a hothouse of unconditional love. The slightest frustration might hurt their feelings and endanger their emotional growth. More recently, the permissiveness of the 1960s is giving way to a tougher approach. Some toughness sounds good to many parents today, who are fed up with the child-centred household that is wall-to-wall toys and crayon marks. Yet today's parents are also enjoined to have *fun* with their children, or else . . .

Like the pendula of most social changes, the swing from permissiveness to law and order can go too far. If we really followed some of the advice books, the home that used to be modelled on Club Med would be in danger of becoming a prison camp. This book is based on our middle ground of caring for children: children need both latitude of expression and firmly held limits on their behaviour, in a blend that results in calm patient management. The key is to tailor the child's world to his or her developmental level – what she or he enjoys, understands, thrives on – and to individual differences between children. Chapter 6 describes the development of babies and pre-school children, and Chapter 7 discusses what kind of care children need at each age.

Nightmares about day care

The prospective working mother may have visions of hundreds of young children pressed into a cramped room. Babies are lined up in cots, each vainly crying out for comfort and attention. There is no one to respond. Overseers shout orders to keep the toddlers and older children in line. Is this what leaving your baby in day care means?

In contrast to this nightmare about day care, there are glorious illusions about the salvation of mother care – a baby and her mother snuggling contentedly in a rocking chair, mother laughingly sharing a favourite picture book with her appreciative toddler, who smiles and looks adoringly at his devoted mother. These polar images – and others of their own invention – haunt mothers who wonder about leaving their babies in others' care. How realistic are they?

Fears about the deleterious effects of day care come in three types, according to Michael Rutter, an eminent psychiatrist: that day care deprives children of the loving care they need to develop normally, that it leads to insecure or aggressive personalities, and that it destroys children's love of their parents. We will consider each of these fears briefly in this introductory chapter and more extensively in later chapters.

Poor Little Orphans. The first fear about infants and young children in day care arose from research on orphanages. Old-fashioned institutions in which babies were cared for by many caretakers in an impersonal fashion have been shown to harm their development. Imagine a baby lying day in and day out in a cot staring vacantly at a white ceiling. The only contact that he has with caretakers is to be changed and fed. No one plays smiley games with him or talks to him. No one responds to his social approaches. He lives on a hospital-like ward with many other unfortunates. The caretakers are overburdened by the mere physical care of their many charges. Such babies are not only emotionally deprived; they do not walk or talk at normal ages, either. They lack the necessary social and physical stimulation to develop normally.

Babies need social relationships with caring, attentive adults. Parents who are so unwise (or so poor) as to place their young children in impersonal, institutional care are endangering their well-being, as we shall discuss in chapters on pre-school children and their care. But the kind of neglect that was seen in some orphanages is hardly the typical experience of children in day care. For most young children in day care, the comparison to pathetic orphans smacks of scare tactics. The reasons for such tactics will be discussed in Chapter 4.

Day Care Misfits. The second fear about the effects of day care on young children is that their personalities will be warped. The warping may take the form of antisocial, uncooperative behaviour or of insecure, anxious feelings. Personality distortion is said to arise from impersonal or neglectful caregivers who do not devote themselves to young children's development.

Most experts agree that young children need consistent attention from a few familiar affectionate adults – relationships that are steady, continuing and warm. We talk about these relationships in Chapter 7. Suffice it to say here that *some* day-care situations may not give young children enough consistently loving and ordered care to develop a real sense of security and a happy conformity to reasonable adult standards. Although the research literature is not conclusive on this issue, there is enough evidence about the problems of young children in large groups to make one suspicious about their effects on children's personalities. But one does not have to place one's baby in a large group. There are better options, as we discuss in Chapter 9.

I don't love you, Mummy. Perhaps the strongest fear is that everyday care by others will destroy a baby's relationship with her parents. Not only will the parents be deprived of their baby's love, but the baby will grow up to feel unloved by her parents. Most experts agree that babies need the security of close attachment to at least one person, usually the mother, in order to grow into loving adults. Mother love supports not only emotional but also intellectual development, because only babies who feel secure can explore and learn from their environments. The psychologist Harry Harlow separated baby rhesus monkeys from their mothers and reared them in isolation. In this research, infants without the warm security of mother love huddled in the corners of their cages and languished. They were unable to love and unable to play. As adults, the monkeys were unable to relate to other monkeys, were not sexually receptive, and failed to mother their occasional offspring. According to psychoanalysts, babies learn to love themselves and others by developing a close bond with their mothers in the first months of life. Without this bond, they may never love anyone.

Could the separation of babies from their working mothers damage their emotional attachment to their mothers? Experts feared that babies cared for by people other than their mothers could not develop secure relationships, as babies with full-time mothers do. Parents and experts also feared that babies would form attachments to day-care workers and not to parents. This could mean that babies in day care would not love their mothers and fathers.

Fears about the dilution of babies' attachments to their parents have been quieted by many studies of young children in day care and at home (Caldwell *et al.*, 1970; O'Connell, 1983). Children in day care show the same degree of attachment to their mothers and the same amount of security as children with full-time mothers. This is just as true of children who have been in day care from the earliest weeks of life as of those who began day care for the first time at two or three years of age. After all, working parents *do* spend time with their youngsters before work, after work, and at weekends. Children in day care are not orphans; most often they have devoted parents, who are intensely interested in their development.

Start educating your baby early, or else . . . ?

Parents are sometimes urged to invest great efforts in starting their children's education from the earliest days. Flash those cards with words and pictures, the theory goes, and your six-month-old will learn to read earlier than the other children around. Play Beethoven in the delivery room, and he'll appreciate fine music in adolescence when all the other kids are listening to hard rock. Parents are urged to devote their time with their baby to learning exercises. And what is more it all has to be *fun*.

The worst blow of all, in our opinion, is the guilt trip sponsored by those who claim that infancy determines all later life. Ellen Goodman, the American journalist, agrees:

> Our inadequacy is brought home to us by those wonderful people, the early childhood people. Now we are told that if we don't hang the right mobile over the cot at eighteen months, our children will never get into Harvard at eighteen years. One of my favourite advertisements, which ran in our paper (*Boston Globe*), carried the following challenge from Burton White: 'Will your children remember you for what you did for them or for what you did to them?' I'm grateful my daughter was four before I found out it was all over at three. This has helped our relationship enormously (Goodman, 1980, p. 6).

The idea that very specific kinds of stimulation are required in infancy to ensure outcomes that parents desire is pernicious. It preys on parents' insecurities. Like Goodman, we are both glad that we did not 'know' our children were doomed to failure if we didn't hang educational mobiles and use flash cards with funny symbols. From the way that they have grown up, it appears that ignorance was not only bliss but sanity.

Babies get all the stimulation they need for normal development from the everyday life of the household, as long as they are included in the family's activities. Babies need 'conversations' with loving adults who talk with them, listen to their babblings, name objects for them, and give them opportunities to explore their worlds. Most parents find these activities natural and enjoyable, so most babies get the stimulation they need to develop well. Unless the baby is left alone in her cot all day as well as at night (when it's dark, so what's the point of a mobile?), she will learn plenty about shapes, colours and textures of objects from being around the house with you. We are not against mobiles – babies do enjoy them – but they are not essential to infants' mental development. Besides, mobiles don't talk, laugh and snuggle.

Providing equipment for the baby can be comforting, especially if you feel guilty about how much the baby is missing from not having a Supermum and Superdad. Everything money can buy is one approach to the baby. But you don't of course think that the baby who has every conceivable mechanical gadget in his cot is better off than the one who is carried around the house wherever parents need to be? What's wrong with putting him in an infant seat on the kitchen counter or sitting him on the floor with a spoon and a kitchen pot while you slice apples?

The romance of infant determinism lives – the belief that early experiences have a more profound effect on later life than later experiences do. Will teaching reading in the cot enhance your child's later learning more than the same attention given at a later age? Nonsense! As we will show in Chapter 4, this idea is tied to a particular view of children, and is not supported by research about children's learning. For the moment, suffice it to say that a six-year-old is much better able than a one-year-old to learn to read and that most adolescents eventually learn to appreciate various kinds of music.

Of course, in the time you spend with your baby you can do whatever pleases you both. It's just not as much fun to flash cards at the baby as to play peek-a-boo or to roll a ball back and forth between you. Infancy is *not* the best time to teach conceptual material, which will be learned much faster and in more enjoyable ways in the pre-school and early school years. The baby who needs to be taught and stimulated is, in our opinion, a creation of salesmen who profit from making parents feel that they are not doing enough for their children.

Parents ought to feel more comfortable about the care of their children than some experts would seem to permit. If children were so fragile and parenting so difficult to learn, where would we all be as adults? In our view, most parents function for better rather than worse with their children, and so can most day-care arrangements.

Working Mothers Are Mothers, Too

Whenever a change occurs in the family, policy makers and researchers first ask nervously what harm will come from the undesired change. They assume that changes in the family are dangerous tamperings with a sacred institution. There *must* be bad effects of divorce, absent fathers, unemployed fathers and employed mothers. Social scientists are not immune, after all, to the cultural ethos in which they live. No one asks what good might come of changes in family life that seem potentially disruptive and disturbing. And so it was for fifty years with maternal employment.

What the studies show – and don't show

Lois Hoffman (1983), a social psychologist at the University of Michigan, has charted fifty years of research on the children of employed mothers. 'How badly off are they?' is the theme of most of the research. Sons of employed mothers were claimed to be less academically accomplished, less self-confident, and less – you name it. Daughters were not so badly affected by mother's working, it seemed, as sons. Digging into the research reports, Hoffman found that in fact the daughters of employed mothers were better off in most ways than the daughters of mothers who were not employed outside the home. Daughters of employed mothers were more self-confident, more successful at school, and were more likely to pursue careers themselves. It seemed to Hoffman that these findings had been buried or ignored by investigators intent on finding out what was wrong with the children of mothers in the labour force.

Lois Hoffman argued that daughters might actually benefit in academic achievement, independence and self-esteem by having a model of a competent female in the household, whereas most sons already had the model of an employed father whether their mother worked or not. Thus, a young daughter could be positively influenced in her own career plans by a working mother, while sons might not receive this benefit of having a working mother and might suffer some lessening of maternal attention if their mother worked.

Recently, the American psychologist Urie Bronfenbrenner and his colleagues (Bronfenbrenner, Alvarez and Henderson, 1983) asked parents about their three-year-olds. Employed mothers and fathers described their daughters as more accomplished and delightful than their sons. Mothers at home and their husbands described their sons as better off than their daughters. Overall, mothers' working or not made no difference in parents' descriptions of how accomplished and adjusted their children were, but the parents were more pleased with daughters if the mother worked and with sons if she did not work outside the home. This may seem to be a peculiar finding, and perhaps it will not stand up to other studies. It is consistent, however, with Hoffman's result. Daughters may actually benefit from having a competent role model in the home. Sons, as we shall see, need not suffer from high quality day care. Given the current state of day care in America, we can assume that some of the sons and daughters in both Hoffman's and Bronfenbrenner's studies had less than adequate substitute care. Even so, for daughters the benefits of maternal employment clearly outweighed the disadvantages.

Lois Hoffman noted too that most of the research on the effects of maternal employment was carried out in a negative way; few investigators asked what benefits there might be from increased family income, higher self-esteem for the mother, a less sharp distinction between mother's and father's roles in the family, and a role model of a competent woman for both sons and daughters for their later lives. Moreover, if we want our sons to respect women's rights and achievements, how better can they learn that women can be as accomplished as men than by living with an accomplished mother? But no one has studied sons' attitudes toward women or their expectations about their future wives.

Concern in the US about the possible plight of the children of working mothers prompted a new study by the National Academy of Science (Kamerman and Hayes, 1982). A distinguished panel of social scientists reviewed all the research on working mothers and concluded that there were no consistent effects of mothers' employment on any aspect of child development. Rather, they said, the research has been aimed at the wrong questions (a repeated theme in this book). Maternal employment cannot have a single set of effects on children, because mothers work for various reasons, when their children are of various ages and stages of development, in communities with various attitudes and supports for working parents, and so on. Overall, the Committee concluded that maternal employment showed no effects on children but that, as always, more research is needed. The major conclusion from the study was:

> Little is known about the consequences for children of employment or unemployment. Simple propositions regarding the positive or negative consequences of parents' work cannot be demonstrated and sophisticated ones have generally not been investigated. Child outcomes, where they have been addressed, are conceived very narrowly (p. 320).

The straightforward results of bad emotional, social and intellectual outcomes for children of working mothers were *not* found, but no research can rule out yet unstudied subtleties. All we know is that the school achievement, IQ test scores and emotional and social development of working mothers' children are every bit as good as those of children whose mothers do not work. At some time in the future, someone may find a more subtle difference between children of working and nonworking parents. At present, however, any disadvantages attributed to the children of working mothers are mere conjecture.

Some of the bad press about working mothers comes from cultural stereotypes that are only now beginning to change. Consider the fact that in the 1960s and even the 1970s only a minority of mothers of pre-school children worked. Community attitudes and those of the extended family were against mothers' employment. The experiences of children in day care were given negative meaning by their communities. In the popular mind, being a child in day care usually meant being neglected. While the other mothers are home baking cakes and stimulating their children's minds, the poor day-care child languished until Mum came home from work. Of such images are myths about day care made.

What Do Mothers Do?

We know that the loving exchanges between mothers and their babies, and the conversations between pre-school children and their mothers, are potentially tremendously important for children's intellectual development as well as for their emotional security. But we have no evidence that the children of working mothers are deprived of these important experiences by being with their mothers for a smaller portion of their waking day than the children of mothers who do not work. A recent large-scale study of what mothers actually do at home charted how much time each day employed and nonworking mothers spent with their children (Hoffman, 1983; Ziegler, 1983). The study showed that employed women spent as much time as nonworking women in *direct* interactions with their children. The employed mothers spent as much time reading to and playing with their young children as those at home all day, although they did not of course spend as much time simply in the same room or same house with the children. Common sense suggests that children need to be able to call on adults for help and attention when they need it, but does the helper have to be the biological mother? Probably not. We know from other evidence that children can feel perfectly secure and content with other caregivers. To have the kind of child-adult conversations that Barbara Tizard and Martin Hughes (1984) have shown to be important learning experiences for four-year-olds, children need to be with an adult who is both very affectionate and also very familiar with the child and the child's world. But there is no reason why this should not be someone other than the mother. What children need is a caregiver who is loving, interested, and who knows them well.

Mothers at home do have one great advantage over those who are employed: leisure. As you may know from personal experience, and as the time-use study shows, working women do not sacrifice their time with their children; they sacrifice their own sleep and leisure time. Many a tired working mother bundles the children off to childminder and school the next day after an evening of cleaning the refrigerator. Reading the paper and re-potting the plants will have to wait for the weekend. The average mother who is not employed works fifty hours a week at home; the average employed mother spends thirty-five hours a week on the same chores, in addition to her thirty-five or forty hours on the job (Cowan, 1983). On average, fathers of pre-school children with employed mothers work around the house for twelve hours fifty minutes a week, compared with their wives' thirty-five hours, which added to their regular employment of thirty-five to forty hours makes for a total of about fifty hours a week. These figures are from the US, but the discrepancy between women and men is just as great here. A recent national survey of women's employment in Britain found that 77 per cent of part-time and 54 per cent of full-time working mothers did *all or most* of the housework, and this is almost certainly an underestimate, according to Jean Martin and Ceriden Roberts who conducted the study (Martin and Roberts, 1984). But fathers with employed wives spend somewhat *less* time with their young children than fathers whose wives are at home, probably because after-work time with the children must be shared with the working mother (Hoffman, personal communication, 1983). For full-time mothers, the return of Daddy can be a time to retreat from the fray of child care. For the employed mother, time after work is a precious hour with the children she has not seen all day, before she has to put dinner on the stove, cope with the laundry and crawl into bed.

Coping with Role Overload

All over the world, women work longer hours for less pay than men. This is not the place to detail those depressing facts (but see Martin and Roberts, 1984; Tavris and Wade, 1984. Martin and Roberts show that 85 per cent of married women earn less than their husbands on an hourly basis, and of course the discrepancy in gross earnings is far greater). Many employed mothers' daily lives make sweatshop labour look like a holiday. Time is the inevitable constraint; no matter how efficient you are, you cannot make dinner, eat it and clean up in five minutes flat. Feeding the baby takes twenty minutes, and he can't be hurried. The washing machine runs for thirty-five minutes and no less. Even if you prepare dinner while the washing machine is running, and feed the baby while stirring the soup, there is only so much that you can do to compress the tasks into the available time. Besides, you are probably tired after a day at work.

If you do not have to have the money and you can manage to find part-time work that suits you and your career goals, this does fit in much better with babies and small children than full-time employment. For obvious reasons, a twenty-hour per week job leaves you time to get to the shops before closing time, to read an occasional magazine, and watch Dallas if you wish. Even with a half-time job, women work more hours than the average fully employed man because of their major responsibilities for child care and running a home. If you decide to try part-time work, do not expect to have a lot of free time.

Part-time work also has the advantage of providing some break in the mothering routine but demanding less time away from the baby. Having some activities outside the home, even if the job is fairly boring, can be an important change of pace for mothers. Just getting dressed, leaving the house without carrying a small baby or holding a small hand, and being in contact with other adults are almost giddy experiences for the housebound mother. Working less than forty hours a week at a job can be ideal.

One solution to role overload for the employed mother is to buy as much help as you can possibly afford, even if it means forgoing other pleasures – which you probably do not have time for anyway. Fathers can also help more than they typically do with household and child-care chores. But two fully employed parents will still suffer role overload, even if they divide the work more equitably than is usual in young families. Unless you are on the poverty line, money spent on cleaning help, fast foods, and other self-saving tactics will be money well spent. Fish and chips or pizza a couple of nights a week will not kill anyone.

Labour-saving devices are not time-saving devices (Cowan, 1983). Money spent on the latest electronic wonders may not save your sanity as surely as the same money spent on self-saving devices, such as help with laundry, or an occasional babysitter while you go to a film. Privileged working women know the value of help. A friend who heads a major biochemistry laboratory, and who had four children in six years, was often asked how she managed. 'Who, me?' she replied. 'I leave the house in the morning and come home to a clean house, happy children and a cooked dinner. Problems, what problems?' That case is extreme, but our own solutions were to buy as much help as possible on our respective incomes.

One still needs to 'get away from it all' from time to time. Some of the money serves well as a releaser from perpetual servitude. Some young couples seem to live up to the full extent of their earnings – and beyond – by purchasing labour-saving devices and maintaining a spotless environment. They have no flexibility to buy help or holidays. Perhaps your mental health will stand up better than ours, but we have needed time away to relax from the exhaustion of the role overload. At least consider wise investments in yourself.

Why, we must ask, are working mothers' lives so overloaded? Why are there so few family, community and other supports for heroism? We cannot pretend to address all of the issues about the role of women in our society, or in any other, but we share in this book our puzzlement about the evaluation of women and children in Britain and in the United States. And we suspect that we have much in common with many other societies.

Child Care

If your main interest is in finding suitable day care for your young child, Chapters 7, 8 and 9 will tell you what to look for. These chapters will also tell you why day care can be good for some children. In contrast to the opinions you'll hear from some experts, research shows that having several trusted adults to care for a child can be better than having one. Michael Rutter suggests – and research (to be reviewed in Chapter 4) on children with more than one 'mother' shows – that secure attachments to several people can be an advantage to children. As experienced parents know, young children can love more than one person. In fact, it is probably better for them not to be at the emotional mercy of just one mother. What if she gets angry, as all of us inevitably do? How nice to have more than one adult in this world to trust!

Having more than one caregiver does not mean being shifted repeatedly from one impersonal day-care setting to another. It should mean being in a small, stable group of young children with a consistent caregiver or two, and being at home with parents in the early morning and evenings and on their days off from work. It is certainly not good for young children to have a constantly shifting army of caregivers, none of whom can give sustained interest to the child's feelings or experiences. Being with different children each week can also be disturbing. It's hard for a person of any age to develop relationships with a new group of strangers.

Child-care arrangements

Basically there are four different kinds of child-care arrangements: mother, father or other relatives at home; babysitter at home; childminder; and group care – day nurseries, schools or playgroups. Although one might assume that being cared for by a parent at home is best for the child, this is not necessarily the case. The qualities of good child care, which we describe in Chapter 7, may or may not be offered by parents, who range from attentive and loving to neglectful and abusive. So it is with all child-care situations – some are wonderful and some are awful. Choosing the best care for your child involves thinking about your child's personality and needs, and being informed about child development and what is offered by the setting. Each of the four different settings has its own advantages and disadvantages for different children of different ages.

Briefly, homes are more informal care settings than nurseries, and they offer a different kind of relationship – closer and more stable – between caregivers and children. The typical childminder is a neighbour or local mother who usually likes children and probably has several of her own. Babysitters are more likely to be older women, who are freer to come to your home to care for your child. Nurseries and day-care centres are more likely to offer scheduled activities, some kind of educational programme, and other children of the same age to play with. Nursery schools will have adults who are trained in early childhood education. It is not surprising, given the different developmental needs of babies and older pre-school children, that parents of the younger group tend to choose care in homes while parents of the older ones choose group care if they can find it. These issues will be fully discussed in Chapters 7, 8, and 9.

Is day care bad for children?

A look at the substantial research literature on the effects and, more important, the *lack* of bad effects of early child care convinced Michael Rutter (1982) that most forms of parenting and day care are safe for children. We agree wholeheartedly with his summary of the evidence:

> [I]t is clear that early claims that proper mothering was only possible if the mother did not go out to work and that the use of day nurseries . . . has a particularly serious and permanent deleterious effect on mental health were not only premature but wrong (Rutter, 1982a, p. 3).

Good child care is just that – good care. The who and the where are much less important than the what. Each child comes into the world with his own individuality and pre-set developmental pattern. Good child care can enhance development to some extent, but it cannot reshape the entire course of the child's life. Poor care can interfere temporarily with development, but unless the bad treatment is severe and prolonged, even such unfortunates generally recover to become normal adults (Clarke and Clarke, 1976; Kagan, 1980). Given good care, children grow up to be themselves – their own unique combinations of genes and experiences. You cannot claim credit or blame yourself for all that your child will become. You simply do not have that much power to alter your child's developmental pattern. Providing good care for your baby is important to her and to you, but excessive worry about being apart from your baby while you work is a legacy of another era.

CHAPTER TWO

Why Should It Be So Hard?

Working Mothers Today and Yesterday

Women need hardly be told that the 1970s and 1980s have seen a revolution in their roles. Not only are more mothers working, but they are working at more diverse jobs – engineering, law, bus driving, postal delivery, and other 'male' jobs. True, women are still clustered in the pink-collar occupations of teaching, office work, nursing and the like, and women's job and income opportunities are still far below those of men. But the sheer range of employment would stun the liberated woman of the 1920s.

The statistics of women's employment show the dramatic increases in the numbers of working mothers. One might think that most of the employed women were mothers of school-age children who could safely leave home while their children were in school. Not so. The increase in numbers of mothers working has occurred among women with children of all ages, including the very young. Between 1961 and 1971 there was an increase of 65 per cent in the proportion of mothers with young children who were employed, from 11.5 per cent to 18.7 per cent. Half the women who had a first baby between 1950 and 1954 returned to work within ten years, but between 1974 and 1979, half the women who had a first baby went back to work *within four years*. The proportion of women working outside the home within six months of giving birth has risen from 9 per cent among those having babies in the late 1940s to 17 per cent of those giving birth in the late 1970s. By 1980, 30 per cent of women with their youngest child under five were going out to work. And in one recent national survey, as many as 47.5 per cent of all the mothers of children under five had been regularly employed outside the home for at least some of the time (Osborn, Butler and Morris, 1984).

These figures apply to all families. The percentage of single, widowed, separated and divorced mothers who work is higher, and so is the proportion who work full-time (Osborn, Butler and Morris, 1984; see also Martin and Roberts, 1984). The numbers of divorced, widowed and single mothers working doubled between 1961 and 1971. The proportion of 'husbandless' mothers with pre-school children who are 'economically active' was by 1976 a dramatic 62 per cent higher than the proportion of other mothers of pre-school children (Tizard, Moss and Perry, 1976). Single mothers with children are a financially needier group, and the numbers that have to work are likely to go on increasing. Mothers' reasons for working range from poverty to self-fulfilment, and more mothers are pushed into jobs by the former reason than are pulled into them by the latter.

Does the Government Help?

If the good Lord had intended us all having equal rights to go out and work and to behave equally, you know he really wouldn't have created us Man and Woman.

This is Patrick Jenkin speaking, a Conservative Minister of the Environment in Mrs Thatcher's government (quoted in *New Society*, 7 March 1985). The attitude of successive governments towards working mothers – while rarely as explicitly expressed as this – has been one of censure and neglect, of muddled and hesitant policy. There has been not simply failure to provide adequate services of support to meet the needs of the rapidly increasing numbers of women working, but also a failure even to discuss those needs. Although there has been such a rapid increase in the numbers of women working, and although many younger women expect to stay in work even when they have children (Martin and Roberts, 1984), this is not acknowledged by government, let alone reflected in the kind of provision or support made available. The increase in women working in fact reverses a trend that has lasted 150 years. From the early nineteenth century to the beginnings of the First World War, the proportion of women working in industry declined. In 1851, one in four married women was employed. By 1911 the figure was only one in ten. The broad economic and social context in which this decline of numbers of women working occurred, and the disapproval of working women that developed during the nineteenth century and carried over into the twentieth century, is beyond the scope of this book. The salient point here is that, except for a period of four years in the Second World War, little support could be found in Parliament for any measure that would encourage or condone the employment of married women, especially mothers.

During the Second World War there was a dramatic increase in the numbers of places available for the children of working mothers. By 1941 women were needed to work in industry. The urgent need for provision for children under two was recognized and, under the Ministry of Health, local welfare authorities became responsible for setting up nurseries. From 194 nurseries in 1941, the numbers increased to 1559 nurseries in 1944, taking 71,806 children; a further 135,000 children were catered for in nursery classes and reception classes. At the end of the war, however, government support for nurseries disappeared. The nurseries were aids to war production, it was emphasized, and not social services in themselves. The Ministry of Health had 'sold' the war nurseries as both educationally and socially good for children. It could not, in shutting them down, argue that the nurseries had had harmful effects. Instead, grounds of 'no demand' were put forward. The closures brought anxious protests from the National Council of Maternity and Child Welfare, the National Society of Children's Nurseries, Nursery Nurse training colleges, Froebel teachers, the National Nursery Campaign, Socialist Medical Association and local public health committees, but these protests got nowhere (see Riley, 1983).

A Ministry of Health Circular in 1945 stated the official view that

> The Ministers concerned accept the view of medical and other authority that, in the interest of the health and development of the child no less than for the benefit of the mother, the proper place for a child under two is at home with his mother. They are also of the opinion that, under normal peacetime conditions, the right policy to pursue would be positively to discourage mothers of children under two from going out to work (Ministry of Health circular 221/45).

The opposition that is expressed here to child-care provision for young children of working mothers, and to support for those mothers, has continued in official pronouncements from the 1950s until today. The annual report of the Ministry of Health in 1951 stated that day-nursery places could not be justified in cases where the mother wished to go out to work to supplement the family income, but were only justified 'where children in special need on health or social grounds were concerned'.

The lack of any consistent or comprehensive policy towards the needs of children and working mothers was reflected in the division of government responsibility for education on the one hand, and day care on the other. Responsibility for most provision was moved after the war from the Ministry of Health to that of Education. For working mothers this had two consequences: the age for which any provision was available was raised from two to three years, and school hours and holidays were not compatible with working hours.

Policy on both education and day care was clearly against provision to meet the needs of working mothers, except in the case of extreme or special needs. In 1963, the Central Council for Education drew up a major report under Lady Plowden on primary and nursery education (Central Advisory Council for Education, 1967). It was on the conclusions of this report that the government White Paper on education in 1972 was published (Department of Education and Science, 1972). Both the Plowden report and the Government White Paper make explicit their disapproval of working mothers. The Plowden Committee say that they 'deplore the increasing tendency of mothers of young children to work'. They recommend that nursery expansion should be part time because 'our evidence is that it is generally undesirable, except to prevent a greater evil, to separate mother and child for a whole day in a nursery'. Full-time employment of mothers is not to be encouraged: 'It is no business of the educational service to encourage these mothers.'

After the Plowden Report and the government White Paper, the Department of Education and Science Circular that was sent to local authorities made clear that there would be no government resources for nursery provision. Strikingly, both the 1972 Education White Paper and the Circular that followed made no mention at all of employed mothers.

The story of official and government attitudes to day care is depressingly similar. In 1968 an official committee (The Seebohm

Committee) reported on services for the under fives (Committee on Local Authority and Allied Personal Social Services, 1968). It acknowledged that there was a need for a coordinated policy, that mothers will continue to work and that many children are looked after in unsatisfactory circumstances. It recommended additional nursery places not only for mothers who could not be responsible, but for isolated mothers and those under stress. However the report also comments that 'it is detrimental to the young child to be separated from its mother for long periods'. The Ministry of Health then circularized local authorities to recommend expansion of day nurseries for certain priority cases, single parents and so on. The needs of the local children could be met, it was suggested, by childminders, and by help to voluntary groups. As Jack Tizard and his colleagues (1976) comment, it is child care on the cheap again.

There is, then, no official recognition of the needs of children of employed mothers, and there is no tax relief for child care. Where any justification is offered for the attitude towards provision of support, references are made to the opinion of unspecified medical or educational authorities:

> Day care must be looked at in relation to the view of medical and other authority that early and prolonged separation from the mother is detrimental to the child; wherever possible the younger pre-school child should be at home with his mother; and the needs of older pre-school children should be met by part-time attendance at nursery schools or classes (Department of Health circular 37/68).

The result of this 'policy' is not, of course, that mothers stay at home. It is that working mothers have to arrange whatever provision they can manage, and that frequently this care is far from satisfactory. As to the 'view of medical and other authorities . . .' on the consequences of separation which the government circular quotes – we will look carefully at the evidence for and against that view in Chapter 4.

Support When the Baby is Born?

Although rhetoric about 'supporting the family' has been common from successive governments, families with children have suffered from the changes in taxes and benefits in the last twenty years (Evans and Durward, 1984). Our situation compares very badly with that of parents in other European countries. The only benefit available to all pregnant women is the maternity grant of twenty-five pounds. The size of this grant puts our mothers among the most neglected in Europe. French mothers get twenty-one times as much.

Britain has a similarly poor record compared with other European countries when it comes to maternity leave and allowances for working mothers. In nearly all EEC countries, the maternity leave period is covered by earnings-related benefit payments, fixed at 75 per cent or more of earnings. The UK is the main exception: the leave period is longer than most but over half of it is unpaid, and the paid period is covered by a low flat-rate benefit. In nearly all EEC countries women are entitled to maternity leave on production of a medical certificate. Again, the exception is the UK where a woman must have had at least two years continuous employment with the same employer. In the UK small employers (those with five or less employees) don't have to reinstate women on maternity leave if they can show that it is 'not reasonably practicable to do so'. Other countries have no such exceptions. The maternity allowance is the chief benefit for working mothers. This has such complicated contribution requirements in Britain that it excludes half of our mothers. Those who have been working intermittently, or on pay that falls below the level requiring national insurance contributions (as so many women do) do not qualify.

Parental not Maternity Leave?

One positive step towards both helping women's employment situations after the birth of a child, and encouraging fathers to take responsibility for children, has been taken by the Commission of the European Community. It is proposing that member states should provide for 'parental leave'. What is suggested is a minimum leave period of three months per worker per child that would apply equally to both men and women. So, for example, in a two-parent family, six months full-time leave per child would be divided equally between mother and father, with a part-time option: both parents could for instance take twelve months part-time leave. The two key features of this 'parental leave' are that parents are guaranteed reinstatement to their employment at the same or a similar job after the leave, and that the leave is equally available to women and men. Behind this proposal is a concern to make opportunities for women at work and at home equal those of men, by encouraging sharing of family responsibility and by helping women to maintain continuity of employment when they have children. It has been shown that the interruption of women's employment with a baby's birth has 'severe, negative and lifetime consequences on their income and employment' (Moss, 1985). The Commission of the European Community is clear that 'caring for and bringing up children should be regarded as a joint responsibility of the father and mother'. It remains to be seen what the British government will do about it.

Child Care in Other Countries

The opposition to child care in Britain (and also in the United States) stands in contrast to the policies of other industrialized areas of the world. Other nations have national policies that promote child-care arrangements for working mothers, for whatever historical, social and economic reasons (Roby, 1975). In Scandinavia, Israel, France and Eastern Europe, half to nearly all of the infants and young children are provided with government-subsidized care while their mothers work. Most of these countries are still struggling to provide enough good child-care spaces, but they are committed to national child-care policies. Child care is considered a right for families in which both parents are employed. Most women's rights are not necessarily better protected in other countries than in our own, but the right to be employed – even at half the salary of a man – is.

The care that these other governments provide is, on the whole, very good. Lest you imagine large institutions in which pitiful babies pine away from neglect, Pamela Roby (1975, p. 134) describes children's centres in Europe and Israel as friendly and home-like, with small, informal groups of happy children. Each room is usually connected to an outside play area, and the children may go outside to tend pets, climb and play wherever they wish. For the older pre-school child, some instruction, similar to that of our own nursery schools, is provided. Babies are tended by trained caregivers, who are responsible for three or four children. Roby's picture is one of bright, cheerful centres, not bleak, desolate institutions. Even if the picture focuses on the better rather than the worse centres, other countries do provide adequate child care for the majority of children whose parents are both employed.

More important, in all these countries children's centres are the focus for *comprehensive* service – medical, dental and social. Most industrialized countries have made legislative commitments to the overall developmental welfare of the next generation, whoever their parents may be.

In their survey of child-care policies in European countries, Jack Tizard and his colleagues (Tizard, Moss and Perry, 1976, pp. 120–21) comment that a main difference between Britain and the rest of Europe is

> the acceptance in Europe, both in policy and provision, of the needs of working women with children under, and of, school age. Full day care, for instance, is much more extensive, and several countries have very ambitious plans for this kind of provision, even for very young children . . .
>
> Unlike Britain, many countries provide extensive public support through grants and subsidies for privately and voluntarily organized care and education of pre-school children, often to the same level as that provided for state or municipally controlled establishments. There is no rigid distinction between the public and the voluntary sector which are both taken into account when considering demand, supply and finance.

They note that

> whatever is provided in the way of care and education outside the home is eagerly taken up, so that no country has yet reached saturation point . . . The greatest area of demand and corresponding lack of provision at present, is care for the very young children; and all countries, with the exception of the Netherlands and ourselves, have accepted this responsibility and are planning to expand provision substantially.

Parents in these countries have choices of child-care settings, just as we do. Subsidies are given for care in day homes, for sitters in one's own home, and to centres. Most parents in Sweden, according to Marianne Karre (Karre *et al.*, 1975), prefer centres to day homes, because the parents can

> be sure that their children are cared for by qualified persons, that a check is kept on their health, and that they are provided with correct food, suitable play materials, and fairly generous space in which to play under the supervision of permanent staff (pp. 141–2).

If all centres in Britain offered such advantages, parents could work with less anxiety and guilt, knowing their children were in safe hands in good places. Such is not the case.

The Hope of the Future

In public discourse, children are often called 'the hope of the future', 'our nation's greatest resource', 'our pride and joy'. One might think that the care of children is an important national priority, and that rearing a sturdy and healthy flock of children is so important to the country that those adults who work with children are especially prized too. After all, to do a good job of rearing a child requires a much more complicated set of skills than repairing a TV set, or selling advertising.

On the contrary, adults at all levels of society and in all occupations that deal with children directly appear to be devalued. From nursery nurses to paediatricians, from school teachers to lawyers working with juvenile delinquents, all of us who work with children are paid less and given less prestige than our colleagues who work with adults.

Consider the lawyer who deals with juvenile law, such as custody in divorce cases or delinquency, compared with one who deals with company law. Prestige and money are far lower for the former. Consider the paediatrician and the brain surgeon. Again, money and prestige are less for the former. What is the difference? The paediatrician is a 'baby doctor', which can be read not only as a description of the clientele, but as evidence of taint.

What is more, the younger the child, the greater the taint. Nursery nurses are paid less than primary-school teachers, who are in turn paid less than university teachers. The older the student to be taught, the greater the salary and prestige.

Status in education might seem to go with the complexity of knowledge to be taught. Certainly the contents of the curriculum for college students is more advanced than that of eight-year-olds. But teaching eight-year-olds is a far more complex task than teaching older students, who are expected to be responsible for their own learning. The intellectual and professional tasks of the primary-school teacher are different from those of the sixth-form-college teacher, but no less demanding of professional expertise.

Let's turn to nursery education. Traditionally and today, this field belongs to women. Under-fives are too much like babies who need child care to have any serious status in education. There is plenty of national rhetoric about the importance of early childhood for shaping the minds and hearts of the next generation. But there is precious little reward – in terms of money or status – for women who contribute to the effort.

Many have pondered the low status of work with children and blamed it on the distance of child care from the realms of power and money. We want to propose another explanation. Children belong to women, primarily. Like it or not, we are the sure parent of each child, the parent with the biological connection to the nursing infant. We have come to the conclusion that children, especially babies and young children, are devalued by their close connection to women. In our view, it is the low status of women that has tainted work with children, whether done by men or women.

Many of the direct battles for women's rights have been fought and won. We can vote, own property, file for divorce and claim our maiden names. The *indirect* battles over women's roles are still to be fought. Child care belongs to the indirect battle-front of tax allowances, subsidies for child care, and a national policy for children. It is one of the top-of-the-list items for working mothers. Another is paid maternity leave, which few British women have for more than a few weeks. In most European nations, mothers can have six months at home with their new babies at full or nearly full salary (Roby, 1975). A third expensive item for working mothers is help at home with all the chores that befall married women all over the world. Men are nearly exempt from cooking, cleaning and shopping whether they live in Paris, Belgrade or Manchester (Cowan, 1983). Much propaganda has been made of the revolution in men's household roles; the reality is that a very few fortunate working mothers are so helped.

So it is, we believe, that women's work, maternity leave and child care are hostage to the active but indirect war between the sexes over women's proper role in the society. Battles over how women can work outside the home without sacrificing their children's welfare will be fought in decades to come. There will be battles about the low status and poor pay of typical women's occupations, many of which involve work with children. There will be battles over the legitimacy of child care, its standards, its availability, and who shall pay. One can only hope that these issues can be resolved in the interests of children. They are the human future.

PART TWO

Mother Care

CHAPTER THREE

Changing Ideas about Children and Mothers

It seems natural to believe that mothers are important to their children's development, but the notion that mothers have special and irreplaceable roles in children's lives has not always been with us. Sometimes it has been stressed, sometimes not. Napoleon's views were clear: 'The good or bad conduct of a child depends entirely on the mother.' When asked how moral values were to be improved, he answered: 'Instruct the mothers of France' (Hardyment, 1984, p. 33). Parents from the sixteenth century onwards have worried about their children's health, delighted in their achievements, been concerned over their education, and troubled over difficulties in controlling them (Pollock, 1983). This we know from reading their diaries, letters and autobiographies. But the idea that children had *psyches* that required special maternal care is rather new – a belief that's grown increasingly prominent since the early nineteenth century.

Why did psychologists and other experts begin to stress a special bond between mother and child, one that required her full-time devotion? In this chapter we trace the evolution of ideas about mothers and children through the advice of child-rearing experts. What have the experts told parents about children and their responsibilities to them? If we track the development of ideas about mothers and children, the dilemmas of motherhood today become understandable. The conflict we all feel between being mothers and having careers is based on many assumptions about the nature of children and the responsibilities of motherhood – assumptions that should certainly be scrutinized and may well be questioned.

The Child and Mother Nature

If we believe that children develop more or less by themselves with reasonable protection and guidance, the obligations of parents are far less demanding of their time and energies than if we think that babies require intensive interaction and instruction for optimum development. *Laissez-faire* parents can relax and watch their child develop, but interventionist parents must be constantly involved in programming their child's environment. Theories about children and what they need make a big difference to how we see our roles as parents.

The conflict that a woman feels about being both a mother and a person in her own right is a socially generated malaise, not an individual problem. In our view, the dilemmas of modern motherhood arise from a mismatch between the current realities of family life and ideas about mothers and children that suited the late nineteenth and early twentieth centuries. The conflict is not between being a mother and having a career; it is between one particular set of ideas about children – a narrow and rather misleading set – and today's ideas about women.

The Nature of the Child

Each era, each set of experts, invents its own child. The ideas that people hold about children and how they should be brought up have changed over the past 500 years – through swings of opinion that express broader beliefs about social, economic, religious and political issues, and even beliefs about the prospects of society itself (Borstelmann, 1983). Optimism about the society's future often goes with optimism about child nature, pessimism with pessimism.

Two major themes are woven through discussions of children and child rearing: (1) Is child nature basically good or evil? (2) Do children need careful and detailed nurturance, or is their growth basically programmed by nature? At some times in history, children have been regarded as naturally evil and in need of salvation by wiser, more godly adults. Stern training and even physical abuse could serve to improve the chances of their eventual redemption. At other times, it was thought that children were basically good and could be trusted to grow up according to their own natural development: all they needed was protection from the evils of the world.

The image of the child as good by nature but perfectible through training and education is familiar to all of us. This child is badly affected by poor environments, including inept parenting. Another image – by contrast – is the good child, free, natural and innocent, who can be trusted to grow up largely on his own, and whose genetic heritage assures his place in the natural order. A third child, seething with potentially ruinous impulses, owes his nature to evolution and his perfectibility to parental management – repressive or sensitive, depending on the era. We shall meet all three children in the twentieth century.

Children get psyches

How parents should bring up their children became a subject of increasingly absorbing interest from the eighteenth century onwards. The ideas of the philosophers John Locke and Jean Jacques Rousseau were popularized in the eighteenth century and read by parents and by the medical men who wrote about the care of babies (see Hardyment, 1984). There was tremendous faith in the potential and the individuality of babies. 'None of us has measured the possible differences between man and man,' Rousseau wrote. His words were conveyed to parents, eagerly read, and the instructions to bring up these babies with 'rational tenderness' were followed. With medical advances and changes in public health the survival rate of babies improved and so did public interest in them. This eighteenth-century emphasis on instinct and individuality in babies disappeared from the writing for parents in the nineteenth century (though diaries and letters show us just how much the differences between their children mattered to parents themselves). Now science and religion combined to make child rearing a matter of continual attention, and there was increasing concern with children's moral and spiritual development.

It was mothers who were responsible for these matters, medical and moral. By their good example, mothers were to shape the minds and hearts of the next generation. Strangely enough, however, little or nothing was said about the *psychological* environment of the family. With all the interest in the childhood years and maternal responsibility, the children's emotional response to their mothers was little discussed. *Parental* love and attention were considered (Locke indeed had warned against the dangers of too much affection). But while for much of the nineteenth century the ideal was one of closeness between mothers and small children, the child's emotional attachment to the mother was little considered, and the dangers of separation from the mother were simply not an issue. As recently as 1930 Stern noted instead how quickly babies got used to a new nurse or forgot their parents' departure. Not until Freud's writings became popular did descriptions of infants centre on relationships with their mothers (Kagan, 1983). Two of the experts we will consider in this chapter spoke little of children's emotions; only Freud stressed the lasting import of children's emotional fantasies about their parents, and children's vulnerability to distortions in relationships with their parents.

Mothers Front and Centre

Ideas about mothers have swung historically with the roles of women. When women were needed to work the fields or shops, experts claimed that children didn't need them much. Mothers who might be too soft and sentimental could even be bad for children's character development. But when men left home during the Industrial Revolution to work elsewhere, women were 'needed' at home. Thc cult of domesticity and motherhood became virtues that kept women in their place.

In the mid nineteenth century, experts stressed the importance of mothers as household managers. Mothers had primary responsibility for their children, but they also had responsibility for providing a refuge for their husbands from the corruption of the commercial world (Lasch, 1979). Women were the moral fibre in the family diet. They were responsible for making the home peaceful, harmonious and uplifting for their husbands and children.

By 1830, science on the one hand, with the new laws of the mind set out by the phrenologists and laws of health set out by the physicians, and religion on the other – evangelical piety within the home – together focused a new attention on motherhood. By the mid nineteenth century there was a flood of books on child rearing, and on children's moral and spiritual welfare.

From the mid to the late nineteenth century, both home management and child rearing were considered important, part and parcel of a woman's domestic role. During the nineteenth century, however, children became increasingly the focus of the ideals of Romanticism. A century earlier, Rousseau had emphasized feeling over reason, primitive over sophisticated, natural over contrived, and simple over complicated. The Romantics had stressed children's need for love and the responsibility of mothers to rear them lovingly. As Romanticism caught the nineteenth-century imagination, children became increasingly precious and mothers more and more responsible for rearing them (Degler, 1980, p. 73). Mother love began to be promoted as the salvation of children. The clearest message of nineteenth-century writing about motherhood is that of maternal affection (Hardyment, 1984). It is strongly flavoured with Christian responsibility, but it is affection nevertheless.

At the same time, child rearing came to be considered an increasingly difficult and responsible task. Motherhood replaced domesticity as a cult, but love was not enough. The new idea was that mothers could not trust their instincts to rear children, they needed *knowledge*. The goal of motherhood was to train the young properly to inherit the earth – or at least their corner of it. It was not so much a mother's psychological relationship with her child that was stressed, as her proper example and consistent training efforts to mould him.

The ideology of educated motherhood

Changes in mood about motherhood in the course of the nineteenth century followed shifts in patterns of the social life of the family. In the 1870s and 1880s, for instance, the preoccupation of magazines for women was with fashion, social life and etiquette. Babies were less prominent. Yet towards the turn of the century developments in medicine and science, together with political and social changes, had profound effects on attitudes to mothers and to parenthood. Healthy and educated motherhood was seen as crucially important to an imperial nation, and the ideology of motherhood was strengthened (Lewis, 1984). Readers of Elizabeth Chesser's popular books on mothercraft were told that motherhood combined the twin ideals of personal vocation and racial and national progress. Middle-class women were supposed to embody a morality, chastity and sensibility for the good of their families and the larger society that were seen as inherently feminine. As motherhood became the focus of feminine virtue, however, a new kind of ideal woman emerged – one who learned and practised the science of child development.

With a new scientific interest in childhood, epitomized in the Child Study Movement, and new ideas on heredity as inherited possibilities to be realized or not according to child-rearing methods, the first years of life were stressed as crucially important. The Child Study experts emphasized the importance of observation by parents (ideally, James Sully said, by *fathers* rather than mothers. The mother he said was likely to be 'too involved, sentimental and eulogistic'). And the interest in Child Science grew. Mothers as well as scientists joined together to share information about their crucial tasks. The British Child Study Association was set up in 1894, then the Childhood Society and the Parents' National Education Union.

The call for training the mothers who had the responsibility of guiding the Nation's children – the future leaders of the Empire – through these crucial childhood years came from our leading educational philosophers. Herbert Spencer insisted that 'an acquaintance with the first principles of physiology and the elementary truths of psychology is indispensable for the right bringing-up of children' (Hardyment, 1984, p. 117). Nurses and nannies should be trained, too, and there was a sudden burst of founding training colleges for nannies.

The domestic science of the early and mid nineteenth century that concerned itself with homemaking skills was transformed into child science. Children now held centre stage in the family drama, having upstaged cooking, sewing, cleaning, money management and fathers. Some mothers even wished to live with their children in boarding houses so that their full attention could be on the children, undistracted by household duties.

In America, G. Stanley Hall, the first US psychologist and president of Clark University, was enormously influential with the mothers' movement. He also addressed experts with studies of children and claims of scientific knowledge (we discount his studies today). Hall was the guru of the child-rearing experts in the early twentieth century. It was Hall who brought Freud to America for his first visit and Hall who wrote more than a dozen books on children and child rearing. He stressed children's developmental stages and the importance of maternal management. In addition, he urged mothers to take copious notes on child development, to be (unpaid) research assistants in the grand new adventure – exploring the minds and souls of children. With the scientific blessing of Dr Hall, children became invested with importance, and childhood emerged full-blown into what we know today.

The battle to keep women out of higher education was lost, but women's education could be turned to children's advantage by emphasizing the role of education in proper motherhood. G. Stanley Hall said that the hand that rocks the cradle has more responsibility than that of the corporate executive. Because children's needs change as they develop, the demands of educated parenthood are very complicated and require excellent education. Now women could be college graduates and mothers too. What could be better? Presidents of colleges in America agreed that their graduates would bring grace and education to their homes, a more important task than any other.

> Women cannot conceivably be given an education too broad, too high, or too deep to fit them to become the educated mothers of the future race of men and women born of educated parents. The pity is that we only have four years of the college course to impart such knowledge to women who are to be the mothers (M. Carey Thomas, president of Bryn Mawr College, 1908, Rothman, 1978, pp. 107–8).

The president of another American college, Wellesley, echoed similar sentiments, extolling the virtues of doing everything 'right' – from setting tables and trimming hats to teaching children to read. College-educated mothers could do it all better. And much of girls' secondary education was aimed at their future roles of wife and mother. In secondary-school education it was urged that there should be emphasis on domestic subjects because 'every girl should be looked on as a potential wife and mother' (Scharlieb, 1912).

Among the middle classes it was generally accepted that the role of wife and mother was incompatible with a career. Even Mrs Pankhurst, perhaps our most famous suffragette, only became a feminist in public life after her husband's death. Most nineteenth-century feminists only claimed the right to extend their domestic influence, and to practise 'social materialism' – philanthropic work outside the family. The ideology of motherhood was enforced legislatively (Lewis, 1984): the 'marriage bar' operated in many occupations right up to the end of the Second World War, even though at this stage single middle-class women were accepted in professional employment. Attempts to remove the marriage bar clearly revealed the hostility felt towards the idea of middle-class wives – let alone middle-class *mothers* – working. As recently as 1927, in the House of Commons, MPs spoke in terms of outrage at the 'travesty of nature' that a working mother represented. Even more abhorrent was the image of a father at home looking after the baby. (Note that similar abhorrence was not expressed at the idea of working-class mothers working.) Although by the years between the wars women had the vote, higher education and some employment opportunities, it was widely accepted that the role of mother was *not* compatible with that of employed persons. The groups who campaigned against the marriage bar worked for women's economic autonomy through pressure for birth control and family allowances, to improve women's lives at home rather than at work.

Nothing was more important than motherhood, President Theodore Roosevelt told a gathering of women:

> The good mother, the wise mother – you cannot really be a good mother if you are not a wise mother – is more important to the community than even the ablest man; her career is more worthy of honor and is more useful to the community than the career of any man, no matter how successful he can be . . . But the woman who, whether from cowardice, from selfishness, from having a false and vacuous ideal, shirks her duty as a

wife and mother, earns the right to our contempt, just as the man who, from any motive, fears to do his duty in battle when the country calls him (quoted in Ehrenreich and English, 1979, p. 190).

Why the cult of motherhood? Part of the explanation can be found in Romanticism, part in the better survival rates of children, part in Evangelism and its influence on the family, part in Darwin's ideas on evolution, which made development an important part of scientific theory. Darwin's major work, *The Origin of Species*, was published in 1859. Parallels between evolution and development focused attention on children. Just as species were thought to represent a progression from the simple animal to the complex, moral human, so the development from infancy to adulthood was considered a progression of ever more complex adaptations. Post-Darwinian philosophers such as John Dewey emphasized the child's educability, an idea similar to the earlier moral redemption through training, with the addition of Romantic notions about the unspoiled goodness of mother nature (Borstelmann, 1983). Whenever children were seen as redeemable and educable, mothers had a special role to play.

One of the most important forces behind the cult of motherhood in the early twentieth century was concern about the quality and quantity of the race. Policy makers saw it as in the nation's interest to extend maternal and child welfare services. The state had 'neither womb nor breasts', and therefore must increase protection for those who did. Child and maternal health clinics and kindergartens were founded; protective legislation attempted to remove children and women from the labour force. A woman who worked outside the home could not look after her child properly, it was argued. Indeed, infant mortality was held to be primarily due to working-class women going out to work.

The mother and the state were dedicated to pursuing the best interests of the child. (Few were interested in the mother as a person.) And the mother was assisted in her child-rearing tasks by a wealth of opinion about the nature of the child and proper upbringing. Mothers had a special role, but needed expert guidance. Three experts, each with his own assumptions about the child, came forth to tell parents how to rear their children.

Three Experts on Child Rearing

The study of child behaviour began a new phase in the early twentieth century. To illustrate the different children that one can invent, depending upon one's predilections, let us consider the developmental psychologies of three experts: Arnold Gesell, John Watson and Sigmund Freud. Each of these men held a different view of child development. Their common attitude which accorded with the attitude of the child-study movement, was that child development could be the proper object of scientific study. Of course, science proceeds from values and assumptions, so each created a child and child-rearing advice to fit his own theory.

All three were influential child experts from the 1920s to the 1940s and their influences pervade our current cultural assumptions about children's natures and parents' responsibilities. Their assumptions and advice to parents are profoundly different, but each is reflected in current attitudes to child rearing in Britain.

Arnold Gesell

Gesell and Watson represent the two polarities on each of the issues described earlier. Gesell's child is good by nature and endowed with self-propelled maturation; he is largely unaffected by details of parental caregiving, as long as it is not abusive or terribly neglectful.

> It is the hereditary ballast which conserves and stabilizes the growth of each individual infant . . . If it did not exist, the infant would be the victim of flaccid malleability, which is sometimes romantically ascribed to him. His mind, his spirit, his personality would fall ready prey to disease, to starvation, to malnutrition, and worst of all to misguided management (Gesell, 1928, p. 378).

Gesell's child is not so malleable as to be thrown off course by parents' 'misguided management', because she has internal direction. Gesell's child is shaped by nature to grow up without much fuss by the parents. Child development is in fact so predictable that Gesell was able to publish norms or standards for behavioural development, much like those for physical growth – height, weight and head circumference. Norms for language, motor, social and adaptive development (self-help, practical skills) told parents that the average six-month-old could reach for objects, that nine-month-olds babble in consonant-vowel combinations (Ma-ma, ba-ba), that two-year-olds stack blocks, and that three-year-olds name many parts of the body. Although Gesell did not intend them as rigid standards, his average developmental norms were used by parents to judge the progress of their children, without regard for the range of individual differences.

Gesell's descriptions of normal development were so successful that they formed the basis for his developmental test which is still used today. The 'Bayley Tests of Mental and Motor Development' and the 'Denver Development Screening Test', used by nearly all paediatricians, follow Gesell's ideas closely and even use many of his items. The tests serve well to identify at early ages children who lag seriously behind 90 or 95 per cent of their age-group.

Gesell recognized and respected individual differences. His norms were meant to convey a description of average development. Children within a normal range but ahead of or behind their peers are not necessarily advantaged or disadvantaged. The baby who walks first is no more likely than another to be the first across the finish line at the London Marathon. The child who talks first will not necessarily become the school debating champion. Children who walk and talk later have just as good a chance of winning. Children have different developmental patterns that deserve respect from parents and others.

> The inborn tendency toward optimal development is so inveterate that he benefits liberally from what is good in our practice, and suffers less than he logically should from our unenlightenment. Only if we give respect to this inner core of inheritance can we respect the important individual differences which distinguish infants as well as men (Gesell, 1928, p. 378).

Gesell had so much confidence in children's inborn tendency to the best development possible that he even proposed that children profit a great deal from good parenting but suffer little from parent's mistakes. The contrast with Watson could not be greater.

John Watson

Unlike Gesell's robust maturer, Watson's child is shaped entirely by nurture, as a passive recipient of detailed training. Watson's newborn is a

> lively squirming bit of flesh, capable of making a few responses . . . Parents take this raw material and begin to fashion it to suit themselves. This means that parents, whether they know it or not, start intensive training of the child at birth (Watson, 1928, p. 46).

Gesell's robust child matures as the genetic programme directs, while the environment plays a supporting role. His child can blossom in many different gardens, and Gesell reassured parents that they could hardly go wrong. By contrast, Watson's child is a blank page to be inscribed by carefully programmed detailed training. In the same year (1928), the two experts offered parents totally different guidance.

Watson, the father of behaviourism, impressed parents with the importance of their responsibilities and the many ways they could spoil their children's development. First and foremost, they must train the child to be a proper adult. Training the baby took many forms. Strictly scheduled feeding was intended to shape the child to the parents' will. Never, never feed the baby when she demands it, or she will get the idea that she controls the parents. Never pick the baby up when he is crying, only when he is being pleasant. Early toilet training, beginning in the first months of life, was similarly designed to bend the child to the parents' will. Later, table manners and other social graces were to be taught to make sure that the child was properly shaped.

Watson's ideas were attractive to parents because he promised that one could make of one's child whatever one wished. This idea fits nicely with democratic ideals of everyman, latent genius and millionaire. Watson's child did not have to make it on his own, but could have a future determined by diligent parents. Anyone, he said, could shape a child into a mathematical genius or a lyric poet, if only one tried hard enough and was consistent enough in training. Latter-day Watsonians include the gourmet baby trainers, who promise you an Oxbridge graduate if only you will buy their products and follow their prescriptions.

In addition to the rigour and diligence that parents must show, Watson insisted on objective and impersonal management of children. None of this mawkish sentimentality that led parents to forget long-term goals and indulge in the temporary pleasures of affection.

> There is a sensible way of treating children. Treat them as though they were young adults. Dress them, bathe them with care and circumspection. Let your behaviour be always objective and kindly firm. Never hug and kiss them, never let them sit in your lap. If you must, kiss them once on the forehead when they say goodnight. Shake hands with them in the morning. Give them a pat on the head if they have made an extraordinarily good job of a difficult task. Try it out. In a week's time you will find how easy it is to be perfectly objective with your child and at the same time kindly. You will be utterly ashamed of the mawkish, sentimental way you have been handling it . . . (Watson, 1928, pp. 81–2).

Watson's child-rearing advice came out of a Victorian era of stern habit training. Although he did not dwell on sexuality, the regimen he set up for parents would preclude any pleasure seeking on the child's part. The parents must dominate the child and direct his interests in profitable directions.

To be the parent of Gesell's child is like looking after a garden of tulips. You plant the bulb in good soil, water it and wait for spring. Each flower will emerge with a predetermined colour, size, form and substance. There is nothing you can do to change the flower's development, except to make it larger or smaller by tending it carefully or carelessly; the basic pattern of the tulip's development is set in the bulb. Similarly, with the joining of the human sperm and egg, the pre-set developmental pattern of a human individual begins. The parent's good care serves to make the child the best version of himself.

To be the parent of Watson's child is like building a house. The builder can design it to be small or large, Tudor or modern in style. The amount of investment the builder makes in its size, architectural details and furnishings determines how grand a house it is. Once the blueprints are set, however, the builder cannot deviate from the plan, or the building may fail. Suppose that he makes the door openings too big – the doors would not fit. The plan for the house can be almost anything the owner wants, but once set it must be rigorously followed. And so Watson said it was with child rearing.

Gesell believed the child to be a biological organism, shaped by evolution to develop into a normal adult – with a little support from the parents. Watson believed the child to be a ball of clay to be moulded as the parents wished, if they were determined enough to shape the child to their wishes. Whereas Gesell stressed that parents should enjoy observing their child's development, Watson stressed the parents' responsibility to shape the child into a proper adult. No more diametrically opposed views of child rearing could have been offered at the same time in history – until Freud came along.

Sigmund Freud

At the same time that Gesell and Watson were promoting their opposite views of children and parenting, a new era was dawning in Vienna. Sigmund Freud invented a child whose image was to infiltrate much of the mid- to late-twentieth-century writing on children and parenting. Freud's child is neither a trustworthy well-endowed maturer nor a blob of putty that requires moulding. Freud's child is a surging mass of conflicts set in time bombs.

> Unlike Watson who brought the hope of Everyman pianist, poet, and King; or Gesell lauding Growth as essentially benign, Freud's picture of the child was uncompromisingly a picture of conflict. No matter how strong the forces of growth or how well-intentioned and informed his parents, Freud's child must inevitably face the confrontation of his wishes, unbearable to his parents and eventually unbearable to him, with the facts of the world (Kessen, 1965, p. 269).

Freud's child is sexually driven and inevitably in conflict, both with adults who seek to curb his excesses and to socialize him, and with himself. Through mysterious processes of learning, called identification and internalization, the child comes to accept social standards and to control his own behaviour, but never without eternal conflicts among what he wants (Id), what he believes to be right and wrong (Superego), and what he considers the most adaptive course (Ego).

The notion of dangerous infant impulses did not start with Freud.

The Victorian era was full of concern about the dangers of unbridled lust, in children as well as in adults. It was a period of fearful fascination with sexuality. Parents were advised to beware of the natural depravity of children, who seek sexual pleasures that will ruin them if they are allowed to develop unchecked.

Freud focused on the origins of sexuality which, in his view, begins at birth. Infantile sexuality shows itself in the oral behaviour of the infant. Sucking and mouthing are evidence of the sexual drive seeking gratification through the mouth. Too much or too little oral gratification leads to personality disturbance. Weaning is the child's first of many inevitable conflicts with social norms. In Freud's view, infants desire to be suckled forever, coming into conflict with the social norm of weaning at around a year of age. As a mother enforces weaning, the baby feels rejected by the only love in his life. Later sexuality is said to be invested in the anal region. Toddlers inevitably come into conflict with parents over toilet training – society's will over the baby's sexual gratification. Both lack of training and harsh training were said by Freud to be sources of personality disturbance.

Finally, in the pre-school period, the male child becomes phallic, his sexuality expressed through his penis. He wishes to express his sexuality directly towards his mother (Oedipal conflict) but is fearful of the wrath of his overpowering father, who owns his mother's body. To avoid a terrifying confrontation and loss of father's love, the little boy renounces his desire for his mother's body and vows to become big and strong like his father so that he can have a woman like his mother when he grows up. The family triangle is more like a noose for the Freudian boy.

Freudian girls were supposed to fall in love with their fathers (Electra complex), experience penis envy, and decide to identify with their mothers after all. Why all this took place was as vague to Freud as it is to us. He had no satisfactory theory of women's development, which is understandable in an era that cared so little about women. Male children, on the other hand, were given detailed treatment in the theory.

Unlike Gesell's innocent, evolved little primate who would inevitably become human, or Watson's pleasingly malleable putty, Freud's child surged with perverse energies that must be controlled.

Inherent in the struggle to curb the child's dark nature was a Catch 22 – neurosis came from too much control, character defects from too little. Few parents could produce mentally healthy children, because child rearing was made a nearly impossible task.

Advice to Parents: What Kind of Child Do You Want to Rear?

Although Freud began to publish on psychoanalysis in the late 1890s, the implications of his theories for child development were hardly discussed by the baby-care writers between the wars. But even though Freud wasn't mentioned openly, hints that his influence was being felt are there in the manuals written from the 1920s on. Masturbation and jealousy for parental love began to be discussed differently; there's some hesitation about early toilet training, and most importantly the psychological well-being of the child begins to be presented as the mother's responsibility. Susan Isaacs, for instance, began to talk of hate, love and jealousy within the family, of childhood fantasies and fears of rejection. Here is Mrs Hartley, author of *Mother and Son*, urging her readers in 1923 to recognize the Freudian child:

> We have set up an entirely false conception of the child to which we cling most desperately. We want to see the child as an angel. We cannot easily surrender the picture of childhood as a period of delightful ignorance and happy innocence. Yet the reverse is true. The child is nearer to the savage than to the angel.

As Christina Hardyment comments:

> The status of the child clearly took a backward step in the 1920s. Having struggled up from child of nature to innocent babe, trailing clouds of glory, and finally to prodigious, much studied genius in the 'century of the child' epoch, the baby now slid back to unpredictable, coarsely motivated savage (Hardyment, 1984, p. 200).

But Freud's child was not popular until the late 1950s. Only a minority of psychologists embraced Freud's vision of children, so that popular child-rearing advice was less saturated with the child-in-conflict than with Watson's habit training and Gesell's developmental norms with which to gauge your child's progress. Not until the middle of the twentieth century did Freud's conflicted child gain prominence in the press and in clinical circles. The Great Depression and the Second World War were barren grounds for the growth of permissiveness and introspection.

The Freudian child who reached the widest British audience was the child of Melanie Klein's vision – a child who was 'inherently flawed', innately aggressive, greedy, suffering persecutory anxieties and frustrations all focused on the mother. The drama of the Kleinian child's development has only two actors – mother and child. But these two actors are so intensely engaged with each other during infancy that it was not possible, she held, to describe an infant without describing its mother. Ironically, although her theory was relatively unconcerned with the impact of *how* mothers behaved with their children, her followers in Britain were eagerly and centrally concerned with how parents should rear this struggling, frustrated child. Most important was D. W. Winnicott, a paediatrician and child analyst who reached a wide audience with a series of broadcasts in 1944, and popular books. For him, mother and child were a single unit, and the all-importance of the mother is a dominating theme in what he said and wrote. Although Winnicott was talking to reassure mothers, the child he described was alarmingly full of wild and conflicting emotions (Riley, 1983). The imagery is full of wild beasts: the child 'has raging lions and tigers inside him' . . . And the message for mothers who might consider leaving the child to work, was, as we'll see, an unequivocal one: don't.

More watered-down versions of psychoanalytic theory appeared in the 1950s under the guise of permissiveness, the view that children would be free of conflict if their good little natures were allowed to develop undistorted by society's demands. (Ironically, no view could have been further from Freud's. He certainly did not believe that children's natures were good or that they should be given permission to vent their raw feelings.) Unsocialized monsters who dominated the household with crayoned walls and jam-smeared furniture appeared as cartoons in newspapers and magazines. Parents cowered in corners, fearful of daunting the child's spirit. Although the social upheavals of the 1960s and 1970s were often blamed on young people alleged to have been reared too permissively, it is unlikely that many parents followed this advice any more literally than they followed the strict habit training that Watson proposed.

Why Can't They All Agree?

How did these dramatically different views of children affect the advice given to parents from the 1920s onwards? Each of our experts has had an audience ready to accept his advice in this century. Each one speaks to a different constituency, dubbed by us as the Arrived (Gesell), the Respectable (Watson) and the Struggling (Freud).

Gesell's child is guaranteed a place in the sun by his own safe healthy growth, which guides him without error towards adulthood – a self-assured, even aristocratic version of development. Parents of the Gesellian child can relax and enjoy parenting without guilt. No matter what they do, their child has Arrived just by being born.

Watson's child needs constant nurturance in the details of development, but she is perfectible. Anyone (however unlikely) could rear a brilliant and perfect child by sheer dedication and effort. Respectable, middle-class parents found his view enormously appealing, because he spoke to the virtues of personal responsibility and individual achievement. Watson's perfect child had respectable parents who would guarantee their child's right to the status they had achieved. Democratic optimism throughout the ages has produced an image of children as good by nature and perfectible through training and education – the child of John Watson and American behaviourism. It is Watson's child who has been favoured by social scientists of this century, until recently.

> The underlying belief in the inherent (or at least potential) goodness of the child, and in the vulnerability of the child to environmental badness (including inept parentage), has pervaded our assumptions about children through the past hundred years, an ideology that most generally captures the child of science. Perhaps, this is in part why we have always lived uncomfortably with the Freudian child, who clearly carries the demon within (Borstelmann, 1983, p. 35).

Freud's child comes from the turmoil of a central European culture, a dangerous environment. The child's inner turmoil reflects his cultural roots. His parents must save his soul through psychologically complex management: they worry a lot and blame themselves for his misfortunes. The Freudian child's own psychological traumas are predicted to be so pervasive that he is permitted to blame his parents for his troubles. The child grows up with a diluted version of the message, but with parents struggling to gain control of their lives and the future of the child.

Changing Patterns of Advice

Whatever the currently acceptable line of advice to parents, the personalities of the advisers come through strongly, and there have always been some tender romantics and some more severe authorities. As Christina Hardyment (1984) in her delightful account of baby-care literature puts it, there have always been lap theorists or iron men (or maidens). Yet the swings of opinion that she traces in detail have, of course, also been strong. In the 1920s, John Watson's approach dominated the books. In Britain it was the notorious Truby King who ruled mothers' lives with his rigid habit-training advice, from a behaviourist background shared with Watson. The baby who was picked up when she cried quickly became a tyrant over her parents. Careful training in the objective ways he advised would prevent this disaster. Don't pick them up when they cry, only when they are behaving nicely. And so forth, according to Watson's doctrine.

By the late 1930s and 1940s leniency over the rigorous habit training was creeping in. 'Psychological difficulties' that might emerge over toilet training loom, though most experts still held that 'ever more efficient habit training was the answer'. Masturbation could be a sign that a child was getting too much cuddling from its parents, but we should handle this indirectly and not induce *guilt* (a new idea?).

Further, the 1940s baby was trusted to regulate the amount of stimulation and food she could take safely. In the early period, babies could not tell how much they needed to eat or how much excitement they could take; after 1942 infants were good judges of what stimulation and nourishment they can manage safely. The baby of the 1950s is to be picked up when she cries and played with when she wants to play – or for that matter, when the parents want to play with her. As Christina Hardyment put it,

> The self-controlled emotionless baby, hygienic in mind and body, was thrown out with its icy bathwater. The new model baby was warmly affectionate, impulsive, dependent and (preferably) scintillatingly intelligent (1984, p. 223).

Consonant with the changed nature of the child, the conception of parenthood changed. In the 1914 era, mothers were supposed to be strong, persistent, patient and full of self-control. Later in the 1930s, mothers were exhorted to know how to do a good job of training, in keeping with the Watsonian message:

> The parents had to use the right techniques to impose routines and to keep the child from dominating them (Wolfenstein, 1955, p. 173).

By the 1950s, parenthood and childhood had become sources of joy. Fathers were much more involved than before and the dictum was to enjoy the baby. Infants enjoyed breast-feeding, baths, food and play with parents. They enjoyed social contact and conversation with their parents. Parents enjoyed the same activities (or else!). Gone are the fears that the baby's erogenous zones would overwhelm him and his parents. Gone are parental fears about training the infant to be a proper adult. Enter the trustworthy child, the sensible being whose impulses are acceptable and who needs supportive, attentive parents. This is the contemporary child, yours and mine, who owes his nature to Gesell, with a little Freud for spice.

The fully fledged Freudian child never quite appears in the child-rearing advice. But a dominating theme of child-rearing books from the 1950s is the child's emotional growth and the mother's part in encouraging this. The writing of analysts such as John Bowlby and Winnicott did, and still does, influence the way we think about children and child care. Freud's influence is there, for instance, in Dr Spock, who by 1950 had minimized training in favour of moderate permissiveness. In an Americanized version of the message, Dr Spock advises parents to recognize the surging feelings of their children, but he also advises parents to be self-confident; if they trust themselves and their child, everything will turn out all right (Zuckermann, 1985). Like most popular contemporary experts Spock enlivens the trustworthy Gesell child with a dash of Freudian conflict to achieve the child of our times.

Today's Child

Most contemporary developmental psychologists who have studied children in a systematic way share the view of the robust, biologically organized child (Cairns, 1983). Today's child is sensitive to good and bad environments, but is resilient. Bad experiences do not necessarily have permanently damaging effects, nor good experiences permanently beneficial ones. A bad childhood can be overcome by later good experiences; a good childhood cannot inoculate one against the traumas of an unfortunate adulthood. Today's child is not a china doll who breaks under the first environmental blow. Rather, our child is a tougher plastic doll; she resists breaking and recovers her shape, but she can be dented again by later blows.

According to most contemporary views, the development of our present-day child proceeds smoothly according to the internal biological plan, as long as the environment is supportive. But just how supportive and how specific do good influences have to be to promote optimal development? Arguments among child-development experts centre on the degree to which development is influenced by the details of everyday life – a version of the Watson-Gesell debate. Some experts are convinced that specific environments have very important effects at some periods of development (Wachs and Gruen, 1982). Language, for example, may be influenced by the amount of dialogue between adults and young children, so that children who do not experience a lot of conversation with adults may not develop as complex speech as those who do. Because correlations among good events are often confused for causation (as explained in Chapter 7), other experts are dubious about the importance of the details of a child's upbringing.

Still other, more Gesellian psychologists stress the importance of the child's biological organization and the individual differences in developmental patterns that determine most of the ways children develop, as long as they have reasonable environments. We argue that parents can and do have important effects on their children but that most middle-class families provide adequate care for their children to develop normally, even optimally.

Some psychologists, such as Urie Bronfenbrenner, focus on the broader social and economic context in which children live and grow. Parents, for example, can devote only as much time to their children as their jobs and other responsibilities will permit. Parenting is sensitive to external demands, so that we must be concerned about families who may not be able to provide adequate environments for their children. The broader ecology of child rearing may have important effects on children's development that are not noticed when we focus only on the child's immediate family. There is little disagreement about the importance of this ecological focus on child development today.

Today's experts are more sanguine about child development than the Watsonian and Freudian experts of a generation ago. All acknowledge the child's biological development, and differ only on the degree to which specific parental practices can influence the child's course of development. The more Watsonian experts agree that the biological organization of development is important; more Gesellian experts agree that the environments of the child must be reasonably supportive or the child will not flourish. Thus, the differences are in emphasis, not in basic conceptions of the child.

But – although this picture reflects the views of the people who study children in detail, it does not reflect the image that some of those who write the 'baby books' portray. Our resilient child is hardly the same as the child that Penelope Leach describes in *The First Six Months* (Leach, 1986). That child is vulnerable to so many things – from nakedness and noise to separation from the mother. If we believe in Leach's fragile creature, we must believe in the dangers (and the wickedness) of mothers' working. But surely we should take account of what the balance of the research into the nature of babies and their vulnerability tells us? As we will see in this book, what we learn from the wealth of this research that has been carried out is that babies are *not* the desperately vulnerable creatures described by Leach. The story of babies' fragility simply does not fit with what we know from careful research. There is no basis, in good research, for a fable that plays so disturbingly with mothers' anxieties and guilts. To suggest that there is does a disservice to all mothers and babies.

It is hard to imagine that parents *ever* followed Gesell's, Watson's or Freud's advice to the letter. Children reared in the casual Gesellian manner would make modern parents nervous – would they be doing enough? Children reared according to Watson's doctrine would have no hearts, and those reared by Freudian dictates (if taken literally) would be thrown out of school for misconduct. We suspect that most parents of this century gave their children affection, training and freedom in moderation – broadly, the advice of contemporary experts.

Current conceptions of children and mothers are part of the cultural ethos of our world. Today's child requires less intense parenting to achieve optimum development than the pure Watsonian child. But today's child needs more attention to detail than the pure Gesellian child. Given the continuing concern with children's welfare and the legitimate concern with women's rights and roles, the semi-Gesellian child seems a good image of the 1980s offspring. There are no timeless truths here – just appropriate ways to rear children in our own time and place.

This journey through conceptions of children and parenthood is intended to alert us to the fact that ideas about the nature of children and good parenting change and conflict. What is good may change with social and economic conditions, because children must live in a society, and society changes. Training for obedience and compliance may serve one society or segment of society quite well. Letting the little spirits loose can suit another. Trusting children to develop along their own normal course fits another time and place – our own, we suggest.

Parents can be dizzied by the seemingly conflicting views of children and advice about their rearing. Change has been more rapid in the twentieth century than ever before; thus, we have greater changes in advice to parents from 1914 to 1984 than in the preceding seventy years. In each period, in each society, children are supposed to be different beings. In part they are all of the things that have been said. And parents can rear them with greater and lesser amounts of training or permissiveness, trust or mistrust of their natural tendencies. To some extent, parents can choose a view that suits their time and place. In the next chapter, we discuss the guilt that arises from Freudian ideas about parenting that do not suit a working mother's life very well.

CHAPTER FOUR

Psychology to Keep Mothers at Home

In the hospital delivery room, the new baby cries, the doctor smiles in relief, and the nurses busy themselves with the clean-up. Father gazes in stunned appreciation of the arrival of his first offspring. After the umbilical cord is clamped, the nurse quickly lays the newborn child on its mother's belly to begin a magical process called *bonding*.

So in the 1980s begins a relationship between a new mother and her baby. No self-respecting hospital would do it otherwise since Marshall Klaus and John Kennell (1976) told the world that mothers who formed bonds with their infants in the first hours after birth were better mothers to them for years afterwards. As popularly understood, the idea of bonding meant that mothers deprived by illness or hospital procedures from the bonding experience were not destined to be as attentive or loving to their babies as mothers who shared with their babies the first hours after birth.

Eight months later, little Sally is crawling around the house following her mother from room to room. Suddenly, the baby looks up from her toys to discover that mother is not in sight. She breaks into tears and wails loudly, as though she has been deserted forever by the one source of security in her life. Upon hearing the pathetic cries, her mother returns from the next room, scoops Sally up into her arms and comforts her, telling her she is a silly baby to have been so miserable when her mother was just in the next room. Sally snuggles and begins to relax. Her sobs give way to smiles and she motions to be put down with her toys. Play resumes, though Sally checks from time to time to make sure her mother is still in sight.

This scene is repeated millions of times per day all over the world. Infants come to know their caregivers, usually including their mother, by the time they are four to five months old. By seven to eight months they often show strong preference for one or a few caregivers, again usually including the mother. This preference, and the associated protests when the person departs, is called *attachment*. Mothers who experience intense separation distress from their babies are often unnerved. How can a momentary separation seem so devastating to the baby? Does this mean that you can't go to the bathroom alone, never mind go to work, without destroying the baby's psyche?

Mothers and Babies: Special Relationships

These two related concepts, bonding and attachment, have been used in recent years to describe good relationships between mothers and their babies. Bonding refers to the powerful emotional tie that mothers can feel for their young. The expression 'ferocious as a mother bear' conveys the image of a mother who will defend her young against all dangers. Among many mammals, such as rats and guinea pigs, mothers who have just given birth learn quickly to identify their own infants, largely by smell. They fight fiercely to ward off predators from the nest and protect their babies. The mothers are said to be bonded to their young.

Attachment is the term used to describe the powerful emotional tie that babies develop to their mothers. Impetus for the attachment concept came from Konrad Lorenz's research on geese. Just after hatching, the gosling looks around for a moving object to follow. The gosling's preference is for a moving, honking object. A shape that has something in common with a mother goose is helpful, too. When presented with a moving, honking, mother-like figure after hatching, the gosling waddles along happily after it. Similarly, lambs follow the mother sheep, calves the mother cow. Among herd animals, where the babies walk within hours of birth, infants are able to identify their own mothers and follow them closely as the herd moves on. (Although attachment to *mother* is not necessarily implicit in the theory, mother is the one who has got all of the attention until very recently.) Attachment in geese and herd animals must occur rapidly after birth when the infants are especially sensitive to such learning. If there is no appropriate mother to follow, geese and lambs will make do with whatever moves; thus, farm children have had attached lambs who followed them to school, and Konrad Lorenz played 'mother' to a flock of greylag geese.

The twin concepts, bonding and attachment, have been used to suggest that there are special qualities to mother-child relationships, not shared between fathers and children or between children and other adults. Bonding and attachment concepts have also been used to give mother a special obligation for her child's emotional well-being.

If a mother is properly bonded to her baby, how can she possibly desert the nest to return to work? If she does leave the baby in someone else's care, she must not have bonded properly. In some circles, this is tantamount to saying that she does not love her infant.

Moreover, if she works and leaves her baby with someone else, the baby's attachment to her is in jeopardy. And the baby's attachment to his mother is what gives him the courage and security to cope with the world. Without it, he is an emotionally rootless orphan. Suppose a mother sheep walked away before the lamb became attached; the baby would surely perish from grief (and starvation). Without Mary the lamb would have been lost. Similar dire consequences are predicted for the human infants of working mothers. If mother walks away, the baby cannot develop a secure attachment. Ergo, mothers should stay home until the magical attachment occurs when the baby is around eight months old. Of course, after eight months of age the baby will protest vigorously if his mother does go to work, because her departure threatens his emotional security.

Every period in history has its favourite tales about mothers and babies. There is probably a little truth in all of them. Whether mothers are seen as corrupting influences on their children or as their salvation (Kessen, 1965) depends more on the times than on the nature of mother-child relationships.

The concepts of bonding and attachment fit conveniently into the notion that mothers have special responsibility for children's emotional development. They give 'reasons' for the notion, because mothers are special caregivers, both because they themselves are *supposed* to have special feelings for their babies (called bonding) and because infants are *supposed* to have special feelings for their mothers (called attachment). These concepts came to human lore from ethology, the study of animal behaviour, but they have served other masters.

Bonding: Hormonal Love

What, you may ask, do rats, geese, and sheep have to do with human mothers and their infants? The concept of bonding came from the literature on rodents, who keep their babies in nests. Rat and mouse mothers are primed by hormones to bond to their babies. The same substances that prepare the mother for lactation also prime her to act protectively towards her babies. She fetches them back into the nest when they wriggle away. She also licks them frequently, thereby giving stimulation that seems necessary for their normal development.

It may be that human mothers are also primed for bonding. The issue is not whether most mothers find their babies attractive and will protect them against predators. The issues are whether this early experience is *necessary* for good mothering and whether it shapes mothering for years to come.

Human emotions have mammalian roots, but each species of mammal has evolved different degrees of mental control over emotional reactions. The human brain is quite different from that of rodents and plays a more important role in our emotional lives. In all mammals, reactions to danger and floods of warm affection are hormonally mediated. In the human case, however, feelings are less hormonally *determined*.

Our thoughts and interpretations of events can also bring about hormonal changes. If we are emotionally aroused by a flood of hormones, we try to think of a reason for our state. And if we think of disturbing or pleasantly arousing ideas, we can become hormonally aroused. We work in both directions, but rat and guinea pig reactions are more closely determined by their hormones.

Thus, rodent mothers' reactions to their babies have evolved as more or less automatic responses. They don't have to think about what they feel, and it's a good thing, too, because their brains aren't designed for contemplation. Rodent fathers do not respond either hormonally or behaviourally to their offspring of a long-forgotten mating, except under unusual laboratory circumstances. Male rats faced with motherless pups will eventually come to respond half-heartedly to their distress. Of course, the pups in the wild would be long dead before father came around to lick them.

Human parents, on the other hand, have feelings that are based on ideas about the meaning of bearing a child. Human mothers may experience some hormonal priming for positive reaction to the newborn. But for humans, unlike rodents, the links between thinking and feeling are complicated and two-way. Thus, the first hours after birth are not as important for human mothers' feelings about their babies as they are for rodents. Furthermore, human mothers' love for their children is far more determined by their thoughts about mothering over the long haul of child rearing. Nature has to prepare mother rats for only forty days of parenthood; humans had better be prepared for twenty years. Hormones just can't handle that.

Primate mothers

Rather than dwell on rodent hormonal love, let us look at closer relatives. Humans belong to the family of primates, which includes the great apes – chimpanzees, gorillas and orang-utans – and the many species of monkeys. There are some more distant cousins in the family, but we won't worry about them.

Primate mothers seem very fond of their offspring. In the wild and in laboratories where mothers and infants are allowed to have normal relationships, mothers carry their young, feed and clean them with tenderness, snuggle and kiss them. The mothers are affectionate and attentive to their infants. They discipline older babies and play with them. Human observers of apes and monkeys with their infants see many similarities between their child-rearing routines and those of human mothers.

There are great differences among species of monkeys and apes in whom they will allow to handle their babies, and how much. Mothers of many species of monkeys are loath to share them with other females in the troop. They fight off the attentions of eager relatives and friends until the baby is ready to explore the world by himself. There are some primates who share child rearing, however. Bonnet macaques pass their babies around to 'aunts' after the first days of life, much as we permit our siblings and parents to handle our babies. Some baboon mothers pass babies around for inspection, because they seem to enjoy others' admiration of the new baby. Sounds familiar.

A model of bonding based on rodents or bears emphasizes exclusive mothering. Fathers do not play important roles in these species. Neither do they live in larger family groups where infant care is shared. If a measure of strong bonding were the degree to which exclusive mothering was typical, humans would seem to be less tightly bonded with their infants than most other mammals and even most other primates.

The evolutionary history of share caretaking in the human case arises from the family group. We do not wander off in the forest alone to have our babies, like chimps who return to the troop only days later. Human births have always been occasions to be shared with other females at least. (Often, the father is not included.) Mothers and other female relatives are expected to help out in the birth and in the days following. Although the new mother has responsibility for nursing, she is typically assisted in child care.

Perhaps exclusive mothering is not evidence of strong bonding in the human species. One should be careful about what species one selects as the implicit ideal for human behaviour. Of course, the appropriateness of the model is in the eyes of the beholder.

The first twelve hours

Before bonding became an issue, hospitals in western nations typically separated newborn babies from their mothers for the first twelve hours after birth. The infant was kept in a nursery under medical surveillance to make sure his condition was stable. The mother went to the recovery room for a few hours and then to her hospital ward to rest after the exertion of delivery. Mother and baby were properly introduced after twelve hours. Klaus and Kennell questioned the wisdom of this practice, claiming that separation after birth could interfere with the bonding process.

In the original research, Klaus and Kennell gave one group of poor, single mothers their babies in the delivery room to hold and cuddle for the first hour after birth. A second group of similar mothers experienced the usual hospital routine of separation from their babies for the first twelve hours. When Klaus and Kennell followed the mothers and their babies during the first year of life, they found that the mothers who had contact with their babies in the delivery room were more attentive and interactive with their babies than those who did not have the early contact. From this evidence, they concluded that mothers bond to their infants in the early hours after birth and that bonding makes them better mothers.

The bonding research has been attempted by others with less success. Although several groups have tried the same procedures, they have failed to find any sustained effects of early mother/infant contact on mothers' attentiveness or devotion to their babies. Research by other investigators (Lamb *et al.*, 1982; Svejda, Campos and Emde, 1980) simply does not show any difference between the affection or interactions of mothers and infants who met first in the delivery room and those who met twelve to twenty-four hours later. It may be that early contact makes a difference to poor, unmarried mothers (Siegel *et al.*, 1980) who are not eager to be parents, but that it makes no difference to better educated, married mothers, who look forward to contact with their babies either immediately or after a few hours. In our view, human bonds are not so fragile that special relationships can be formed only in the delivery room. If this were so, fathers, adoptive parents, mothers with caesarean sections, and parents with sick babies would be out of luck.

Let us look at other evidence about bonding in primates. Apes and monkeys in the wild are not separated for more than a few minutes from their newborn babies, so that it is impossible to know if the first twelve hours after birth are particularly important to bonding, or even if such a process occurs. But other evidence suggests that apes and monkeys, like humans, have far more sophisticated brains than rodents, so that hormonal love does not play much of a role for them.

In the laboratory, infant monkeys have been separated from their mothers for the first days after birth, just as human infants used to be in hospitals. There do not seem to be any long-term, bad effects from brief separation. The monkey mothers seem delighted to have their babies returned. They react with joyous relief and extra possessiveness for some days. Then they settle into normal mothering. Separation for a day or two at birth does not seem to damage a monkey mother's love for her baby.

Why should human mothers be more affected, when they can see the baby through the nursery glass and look forward to holding the baby in a few hours? This is not an argument for separating newborn babies from their mothers. Quite the contrary! Some mothers indeed respond with floods of positive feeling on first encountering their newborn infants in the delivery room. For them it is a moving experience. No one should take that away, even if bonding is not an excuse for the practice. Who knows what the robin feels when the first egg hatches? Even if we're not bonding, we can have feelings.

Immediate contact with one's newborn baby is exciting – a wonderful moment for most mothers. But this early contact or lack of it does not permanently enhance or destroy a mother's relationship with her baby. Your relationship *begins* at birth, or soon thereafter, and many other events of the next years will shape your interactions: when your baby first smiles at you, says your name, or when as a sleepy two-year-old he says he loves you.

Costs of the bonding idea

The current status of the bonding concept is that it is of dubious usefulness to our understanding of parent-child relationships. There is a romantic feel to the idea that mothers can become permanently bonded to their infants at birth, but other important people get left out of the fun. Because they are not hormonally primed, fathers and adoptive parents, in this view, cannot share the special feelings of a bonded mother. As we have seen, however, they have no reason to worry, because the results of the original research have not held up to scrutiny and further studies.

Fortunately for fathers, observations made in the hospital (Parke and Sawin, 1980) show that new fathers are just as attentive to their newborn babies as new mothers. They find their babies attractive and interesting, just as mothers do. Mothers are more involved in changing and cleaning the baby, probably because this is their expected role. Fathers are more involved in playing, because this is *their* expected role. The new parents spend nearly identical time looking at and interacting with the baby.

If bonding does not shape a 'special' relationship, then adoptive mothers do not have to worry about loving their babies. Nor do mothers of premature babies, who are too fragile at birth to be handled and who often stay in the hospital for weeks after birth. Such mother-infant pairs can be just as attached to each other as those who have a more usual birth.

As the biological mothers of seven full-term, healthy infants, and as researchers who have studied adoptive families and premature infants, we were both, independently, bothered by the bonding concept. We have seen too many adoptive parents who are devoted to their children and too many mothers of low-birth-weight infants who welcomed the baby home with enthusiasm after months in the hospital. We have also seen normally delivered infants whose mothers were not enthusiastic in the slightest about getting to know their babies in those first few days. The mother-infant relationship *begins* in the first days of life, but it has a long way to go from there.

Suppose that many women do feel a special affinity to their newborn babies by virtue of giving birth to them, something that fathers and other adults have not experienced. Suppose that mothers who are at home full time develop more intense bonds with their babies. There is no evidence for or against either idea. Even if either or both are true, does this mean that mothers have to stay home with their babies twenty-four hours a day, every day of the year? In the next section, we will discuss why intense bonds are not necessarily a good idea.

Attachment: Precocial Love

The concept of attachment came to us from the study of precocial animals, which humans are not. *Precocial* animals (the word has the same derivation as *precocious*, suggesting early maturity) are those, like sheep and geese, that follow their mothers within hours after birth. So that they will not get lost, evolution has equipped them with a quick learning scheme. The internal instruction is, 'Follow the first moving, motherlike thing you see and hear.' In the wild, the first moving, motherlike thing a precocial baby encounters is very likely to be the mother. This evolutionary solution is especially suited to species of animals who do not keep their young in nests.

Many other species of birds and mammals keep their babies in nests until they have feathers and can fly or have fur and can walk. Nesting animals are called *altricial* (meaning naked and helpless, in need of nurturance), because the young stay in a nest protected by a loyal mother (occasionally a father, too) until mature enough to venture forth. Rats, cats, robins and primates are altricial. Attachment of offspring to their mothers occurs much later in these species. If you had to make a comparison between birds and humans – a rather dangerous leap across the evolutionary tree – geese would not be the most obvious choice. Robins might be better.

Our babies do not have to 'attach' and follow us home from the hospital. We carry them, like all primates in the evolutionary line to which we belong. Primate babies do not become attached to their mothers for some weeks – not until they are mature enough to know one adult from another. If you don't know who your mother is, you can't very well prefer her to anyone else. Between the sixth to tenth month, however, human babies show signs of attachment to parents and siblings, and sometimes to other important people in their lives. Usually, but not always, one of these attachments is to the mother.

Coming from an ethological viewpoint, the psychiatrist John Bowlby (1969) proposed that infants' behaviour towards their mothers should be understood by its functions; that is, what use is it to the child? Bowlby said that the functions of attachment are (1) to provide the baby with a safe base from which to explore and learn about the world, and (2) to provide a safe emotional haven with which to control anxiety and stress. Being close to an attachment figure makes babies feel safe enough to explore and quiets their fears when they are distressed.

Many investigators had attempted to study babies' attachment to their mothers by observing their smiling to the mother and other people, by recording the amount of protest when the mother left, measuring how far the baby crawled or walked towards the door by which the mother left and charting specific reactions to the mother's return. They found little consistency in specific behaviour for the same infant on two or more occasions (Masters and Wellman, 1974). Mary Ainsworth (1973; Ainsworth *et al.*, 1978) concluded that piecemeal approaches did not capture the *quality* of a child's attachment – how secure the baby felt with the mother. She devised the Strange Situation, in which nine- to eighteen-month-old babies are brought to an unfamiliar room by their mothers and subjected to a series of eight episodes of being with the mother, with a stranger, alone, and reunited with the mother. In the Strange Situation the baby has a full range of possibilities to show how he uses the mother as a safe base and an emotional support. The overall rating of the baby's attachment is intended to capture the flavour of his relationship with his mother.

According to Bowlby and Ainsworth, relationships between babies and their caregivers have different qualities. Infants' attachments are classified by Ainsworth and her colleagues into two broad groups with subdivisions. Securely attached infants protest when their mother leaves, welcome her back, and settle into play again. Anxiously attached infants protest when she leaves, are ambivalent about her return, and may even behave as though they are angry by resisting contact with her. Anxiously attached infants cry more at home than secure babies. They protest when they are picked up and put down. Their relationships with their mothers have a 'no-win' quality.

In various studies by Ainsworth and her colleagues, they find that about 65 per cent of middle-class infants in the US are securely attached to their mothers, and about 35 per cent score in the anxiously attached category. Lower-class infants, especially those of young, unmarried mothers, are less likely to be securely attached – only about half behave as though they can use their mother as a secure base for exploration and emotional support.

Ainsworth says that most of the difference in the quality of babies' attachments is due to differences in the sensitivity of the mother to the baby's needs in the early months of life. Mothers who respond quickly and appropriately to their baby's cries of hunger, discomfort, and boredom, she suggests, have more satisfied and securely attached children in later months. Mothers who are slow to respond or who cannot 'read' their babies' signals are also those who seem to have difficulty cooperating with the baby in feeding, bathing, changing nappies, and all the rest. They seem awkward and 'out of synch' in handling their children. Their babies are less likely to feel securely attached.

But this account of why mothers and babies differ in their relationships leaves out, entirely, what the *babies* bring to the relationship. All parents of more than one child know how much babies differ. A number of psychologists have argued that these differences between babies are important in the way the relationship between mother and baby develops. Some babies are easy to care for, because they are relaxed, adaptable, regular in their schedules of feeding and sleeping, and generally pleasant to deal with. Other babies are irritable, jumpy, and disrupted by any change in feeding or sleeping. They become easily distressed, cry for prolonged periods, and are difficult to comfort. Difficult babies are less likely to be securely attached to their mothers than are easy babies, not because their mother is insensitive but because such a baby is very difficult for any mother to deal with.

The best way of thinking about attachment, in our view, is to see it as the outcome of an interaction between two people, each of whom contributes to the quality of the relationship. Most parents can promote a secure relationship with a calm, pleasant, patient baby. Only particularly sensitive and patient parents can promote a secure attachment for a difficult baby.

Attachment and the Victorian view of motherhood

Attachment is a useful concept to describe a real emotional tie that babies develop toward the end of the first year for one or more of their caregivers. The problem is that the ethological idea has been squeezed to fit psychoanalytic views of mother-child relationships. The traditional psychoanalytic concept is that infants *must* be attached to their mothers, or there will be emotional hell to pay in later life. In Freudian theory and its derivatives, mothers are the central figures in children's lives. Failures in mothering are the root of children's personality problems. The failure to trust one's mother-feeder in the infant oral phase (Freud) was said to lead to serious personality disturbance later. This lack of basic trust (Erikson) would leave the infant unable to love or trust others. Mothers who desert their babies to work risk mistrust. At best, infants without firm atachments to their mothers should become inadequate personalities with shallow feelings.

Bowlby (1969) and Ainsworth (1973) subscribed to the primacy of the maternal-infant relationship. Although attachment theory made room for a 'mother-figure', the biological mother was, in fact, the focus of all their attention. In retrospect, they did not need to emphasize a special relationship with the mother, only the universal need of infants (and all other human beings) for close relationships with others. Their research is of great interest without the emphasis on mothers *per se*.

The problem with the psychoanalytic view that only mothers can fill infants' needs is that it is without empirical support. Many studies now show that infants can develop perfectly healthy personalities in a variety of care arrangements, with attachments to people other than the biological mother; this research is to be reviewed in the last section of this chapter. For now, it is important to understand why the mother was promoted as her baby's sole love. To understand this, one needs to see the cultural context of psychoanalysis.

The ideal mother-child relationship in the Victorian era was symbiotic – an intense mutual dependency. Mothers often slept with their children for many years. Father had a separate bedroom. With the intimacy of shared beds, Victorian mothers were probably quite close to their children, and vice versa (Rothman, 1978). In such a setting the Oedipal conflict seems almost inevitable. The Mother's place in the home as the primary, or exclusive, child rearer was the ideal arrangement. Fathers went out of the tranquil home into the corrupt world to earn the family living, while mothers tended the refuge (Lasch, 1979).

Psychoanalysis in Victorian Vienna served as a justification for intense and exclusive mother-child bonds. In one stroke, the mother's place in the home and the father's exemption from child care were deemed not just a compatible arrangement for the times but an eternal good. If babies could not grow emotionally without the exclusive attention of their mothers, then mothers would hardly protest at being kept at home. It was good, right, and the Natural Order of Things that mothers and babies should cling together.

Freud's observations of personality disturbances in his patients did not cause him to question Victorian cultural arrangements, which he justified repeatedly in his theory. His interpretations of mental distress took for granted the culturally prescribed roles of women, men, and children. Like apologists of all eras, he found 'reasons' for individual distress that did not rock the cultural boat.

Cultural perspectives on child rearing

Genius though he was, Freud seemed to know little of family relationships beyond the middle class, and he certainly was not a student of historical accounts of ideal child rearing in other centuries. Although Freud lived well beyond the blossoming of cultural anthropology, which told the world of strange and different child-care arrangements that seemed to produce normal human beings, he was not concerned with the implications of cross-cultural information for a theory of human development.

To understand the effect of Freud on child-rearing advice, we need to recall the fundamental shift in views of children and mothers that occurred in the 1940s. Mothers of the previous decade were supposed to *train* their children to be proper adults, in the Watsonian fashion, and to avoid unnecessary sentimentality. Business is business, and rearing a child was considered a serious commitment to doing a good job. Official messages about child rearing by the 1950s focused on relaxed and enjoyable parenting, as Gesell advocated, but the popular literature became infused with the Freudian message. Books and magazine articles told mothers to love their children above all else. The ideal mother was one who found passionate personal fulfilment in fulfilling the needs of her child.

> She instinctively needed her child as much as her child needed her. She would avoid outside commitments so as not to 'miss' a fascinating stage of development, or 'deprive' herself of a rewarding phase of motherhood (Ehrenreich and English, 1979, p. 221).

In the eyes of psychoanalysts, motherhood is not a duty but, like childbirth and breastfeeding, a biologically given function. The psychoanalysts actually made mother love into an instinct, 'the intangible core of the mother-child relationship, the glue which alone could hold the mother to the child and the woman to the home' (Ehrenreich and English, 1979, p. 221). T. Berry Brazelton, a noted paediatrician and psychoanalytically oriented child-rearing expert, believes that mothers are, in his words, 'fine-tuned' for sensitive child care, whereas fathers and other caregivers are only poor, insensitive substitutes for biological mothers. Furthermore, mothers suffer when they are not with their babies full time, because mothers feel they are missing out on important phases of their babies' development.

Given Freudian assumptions about the nature of children and the biological predestination of mothers, it is unthinkable for mothers voluntarily to leave their babies in others' care, without guilt about the baby's well-being and a sense of self-deprivation. Mothers need their babies for their own mental health, and babies need their mothers for their mental health – a reciprocal and symbiotic relationship.

Lest you think these views are not current, let us recount a nationally televised interview that took place in the autumn of 1983. A pregnant hostess of a television show interviewed a psychoanalytically trained author of a best-selling child-rearing book. The hostess asked the expert if she should worry about leaving her baby with a sitter while she works. The expert told her that research shows that the babies will thrive with good caretakers and that the mother does not have to be with the baby full time. But, he stated, mothers who leave their babies with others while they work inevitably feel that they are missing out on important phases of their baby's development, precious experiences that cannot be recaptured. All 'good' mothers suffer when they leave their babies in alternate care. If you don't suffer, you are, ergo, not a good mother. The interviewer seemed abashed.

Why should working mothers feel guilty or deprived? Working mothers spend four to six hours a day with their babies, rather than all eight to twelve of the baby's waking hours. Are they missing significant developmental phases? Should they 'suffer' from being away part time from maternal responsibilities, if they also have paying jobs that are important to them and to the rest of the family? Being apart from someone you love is *of course* a wrench, and leaving an eight-month-old or a two-year-old can be momentarily sad for any parents, working or not. Every parent has felt that sadness. But it should not be *suffering* – for you or for your baby. Being apart need not mean depriving the baby or subjecting her to stress, any more than it means your missing a developmental stage.

Recent studies show that babies in day care protest against separation from their mothers just as often and vigorously as babies at home full time with their mothers (Kagan, Kearsley and Zelazo, 1978; Belsky and Steinberg, 1978). When separated and reunited with mother and day caregiver, babies at home with their mothers full time and babies in day care showed identical preferences for their mothers as safe bases and as emotional supports. Day caregivers were not preferred to mothers. Both groups had the same percentage of securely and insecurely attached infants.

Why should this result be surprising? Only because we fear the worst, and our fears have been augmented by the experts who brought us mother-infant symbiosis. Think about it. Working mothers who are away from their babies for eight to nine hours a day still provide the majority of their infants' care – before and after work, on days off, and on vacations. Parents also have a special investment in their children that shows in the kinds of responsiveness they have to the baby. Babies respond to sensitivity, as Mary Ainsworth has shown.

However delightful one's offspring, it is a relief to have some other interests and activities with adults to complement the hours of baby talk and spilled food. Most women's careers and work interests do not absorb all of their time and energies, any more than those of most men; both parents can also spend time with their children, and they do. We know that babies develop as well in non-maternal as in maternal care, *as long as the care is of good quality*. The issue is not who gives the care but quality of that care, which we will discuss in Chapter 9. The guilt trip is, in our view, a hangover of another era and of unacknowledged tactics to keep women in their proper place – at home full time.

Psychoanalytically oriented experts are still singing the same tune that Freud composed. Many of Freud's followers maintain an essentially Victorian view of mothers and children. Followers of Freud have opposed day care, because they believe infants must have intense, exclusive relationships with their biological mothers to develop normally. They inflict guilt on mothers who have to or want to work outside their homes. They denigrate the important roles that other adults, including fathers, can play in the lives of infants and young children. In divorce cases, they may even oppose fathers' visits to their children, because young children need intense relationships with their mothers (Goldstein, Freud and Solnit, 1973). In our view, such ideas have retarded social progress for children, women and fathers.

Despite voluminous psychological research to refute psychoanalytic ideas about the necessity of intense, exclusive mothering for children's mental health – and indeed its potentially damaging effects – they cling to the assumptions of the master. Let us examine research on the positive effects of having more than one attachment.

Several Attachments are Good

Can you think of any reason why babies and children should not be encouraged to trust more than one other human being? How can it be bad to have a loving father, sister, grandmother and lady-next-door? Fortunately for common sense, psychological research has shown that babies with more than one attachment are less distressed when their mother leaves to go to work. They are more content and playful in the presence of other adults, meaning that they feel secure with people other than their mother (Schaffer, 1977; Rutter, 1982b).

Infants with attachments to more than one person are also less distressed at the birth of a brother or sister who occupies much adult attention. A child with more than one caregiver is more ready to share attention with a potential rival than one whose only relationship is with his mother. In Cambridge we studied how a group of pre-school children responded to the birth of a new sibling (Dunn and Kendrick, 1982), and found that children with particularly close, intense and exclusive relationships with their mothers suffered more distress and grief at the birth of the new baby than children whose relationships with their mothers were less intense. They were more negative towards the new baby than children who had intense relationships with their fathers and other adults as well. And the negative relationship set up between the siblings at the birth of the second persisted in nasty ways for several years afterwards. Even at six years of age, the older child who hated the new sibling from the first was likely to be fighting and arguing with him more than children who had been more positive and interested in the new baby at the birth. This continuing hostile relationship was most likely to occur when the mother had a specially close relationship with her first child.

Research by Rudolph Schaffer and Peggy Emerson in Scotland and many other studies show that infants most often form multiple attachments to familiar people at about the same time. Schaffer and Emerson (1964) studied families with babies over time to see how the babies came to form attachments to people in the household and to other adults and children with whom they came in contact. Schaffer and Emerson discovered that babies do not always do what psychoanalytic theory predicts; that is, they do not always form the first or even a strong attachment to their mothers, even if the mother is at home all the time. Sometimes babies put up more of a fuss when their father leaves or protest more at the departure of an older sister who is especially fun to be with.

Most often, babies of nine to twelve months come to prefer the company of their mother *and* father *and* grandparent *and* older siblings. They are content to be left with any one of them and protest when any one of them leaves. The number of attachments depends largely on the infant's opportunities to get to know other people:

> There is, we must conclude, nothing to indicate any biological need for an exclusive primary bond (with mother); nothing to suggest that mothering cannot be shared by several people (Schaffer, 1977, p. 100).

In recent years several researchers (Lamb *et al.*, 1982; Main and Weston, 1981) have studied babies' attachments to mothers and fathers. They find that some babies who have anxious relationships with their mothers have good, secure attachments to their fathers –

and vice versa, of course. Ainsworth agrees that babies can have different patterns of relationships with various important people in their lives. Schaffer (1977) sums up current thinking on infants, mothers and attachment:

> Until recently the conventional view of the mother-infant bond stressed above all its exclusiveness. It was thought essential for a child's mental health that his care should be monopolized by a single mother-figure. And, in any case, the child was thought unable initially to form specific attachments to more than one person – and that person was, of course, his ever-present mother.
>
> Empirical investigations have revealed the truth to be rather different. An infant is not confined to just one bond, as Bowlby suggested: once he has reached the stage of forming specific attachments, he is capable of maintaining a number at the same time (Schaffer, p. 100).

Babies thrive on having relationships with more than one person. They feel secure, playful, and happy with familiar, reliable caregivers, playmates and friendly visitors. The human species does not seem attuned to exclusive mothering at all, but to secure relationships with others.

Do mothers need exclusive attachment?

Babies' attachments to others are hard for some mothers to accept. They do not relish the idea that their babies enjoy others' company so much they do not miss their mother when she is gone. At root is the belief that babies ought to love their mothers *more* than anyone else, including their fathers and babysitters.

Perhaps the baby's cheerful acceptance of his mother's absence seems to speak badly of the mother-child relationship. Any baby who loves his mother should *suffer* when she is gone. Hoping to be loved exclusively by the baby is like hoping one's best friend does not have any other friends. Sounds selfish, doesn't it? And to hope that the baby will suffer in his mother's absence is not in the best interests of the child.

Let's look at it a different way. A well-adjusted baby should be happy most of the time. Playfulness, smiles and laughter and cuddliness are good signs of mental health. Crying for long periods, moping in a corner and rejecting friendly approaches from familiar people are not. Infants can be well adjusted to exclusive care by mother, and they can be well adjusted to part-time care by other familiar people with whom they have relationships.

If a baby is accustomed to her mother's exclusive care, it may take her some days or weeks to accept the friendly care of a substitute. If, on the other hand, a baby is used to two or more caregivers, the chances are she will adapt more quickly to another. Like adults, babies do not accept new relationships instantly, but also like adults, those who have several friends are more ready to accept another.

For mothers who need to be employed outside the home, there should be comfort in the idea that babies' mental health can be served by more than one caregiver. If we can just give up the idea that exclusive attachment signals a better mother-child relationship than several attachments, we can feel happy about the type of care we want to arrange. It may help to see exclusive maternal attachment as an ideal from our cultural past, a relic of Victorian women's enforced unemployment.

CHAPTER FIVE

Psychology for Working Mothers

It's seven o'clock on a Monday morning. Everyone in the Johnson household has been up for at least half an hour. Jimmy is getting ready for school, Dad is shaving, and Mum is giving Amy her breakfast. All four members of the household will be out of the house by seven forty-five, on their ways to school, childminder and work. They will return at about six o'clock tonight. It will be a long hard day.

Dad will drop eighteen-month-old Amy at the childminder's house, while Mum deposits seven-year-old Jimmy at the home of a friend to wait for the half-hour before it is time to walk to the local primary school. Father's job as an accountant at a bank requires him to be at work from eight forty-five to five o'clock. Mother's job as a laboratory technician begins at eight-thirty and ends at four forty-five. She will pick up the baby on her way home, stop at the shops for essentials, and go on home to cook dinner for the family. Father will pick up Jimmy from the friend's house where he stays after school, stop to pick up the cleaning, and get petrol for the car before he arrives home . . .

The family schedule is tight, but money would be even tighter if the mother had not continued to work. Both parents agreed that they would all be better off with two incomes, even if that meant having to juggle children's schedules with their own. The margin of safety is slim. When Jimmy is ill, someone has to stay with him. Fortunately he is a healthy child. When Amy has a cold, the childminder will still take her, but no one knows what to do when she gets chicken pox, as she surely will one day.

It is also seven o'clock at Mary Talbot's house. Her three children are getting ready for school and childminder. As a single parent of three young children, Mary needs an income, but she makes only a tiny bit more than she would get on government benefits for the unemployed – and it is a struggle every week to make ends meet. After paying for child care, Mary calculates that she makes about 40p an hour. On many days she thinks that her supermarket cashier's job is not worth the struggle.

With no car, the logistics of getting everyone around the town on time are bafflingly difficult. Her oldest child, Beth, is in primary school for the morning but has to be picked up in Mary's lunch break and taken to a childminder. She has tried to find another mother to share pickups at school, but so far has had no luck. Her three-year-old and the baby will be taken to the same childminder for the whole day. The woman who takes care of the children also takes in four other pre-school children. In the afternoon Mary's oldest child and two other school-age children join the fray in the childminder's living room. There are too many children in too little space, but the minder charges less than many others. It's the only arrangement that Mary can possibly afford. She worries, constantly, about the children.

Working may not be economically feasible for some mothers like Mary Talbot. She cannot afford the kind of child care that her children need. The children might be better off with their mothers at home on the dole than at a crowded childminders. On the other hand, Mary would become hopelessly pessimistic if she had to struggle on the dole. Depressed mothers do not make the happiest homes for children. Damned if you do and damned if you don't.

For families above the poverty line, such as the Johnsons, the dilemmas of mothers' working are not as acute. Rather, there are chronic strains on the whole family, because there are so few back-ups should anything unusual happen. In fact, the usual vicissitudes of life, such as illnesses of children and babysitters, sitters' holidays, and school and bank holidays, can cause chaos in the lives of working parents. Meeting the working hours of doctors, dentists and piano teachers is nearly impossible.

Grandparents live hundreds of miles away. Often they both work, anyway. Other mothers of young children are also employed. There is no one to care for the sick children, so that working parents have to take precious vacation days to care for them. This means fewer days to share at leisure. When the children are young, families need frequent help from others. In the final chapter, we will consider some ways such assistance could be arranged.

In addition to the difficult logistics of working and arranging suitable child care, many working mothers carry heavy psychological loads. Mothers often feel that their children are not getting the quality of care that they themselves would provide if only they could stay home. Sometimes it is realistic, as in the case of the working poor. Sometimes it is not.

Even if mothers enjoy working and feel they would go crazy without an adult life at work, many still feel guilty that they may be sacrificing their children's interests to their own. These fears may not be realistic dangers for children but rather hangovers from Victorian psychology, discussed in Chapters 3 and 4. The monetary cost of working can be measured in the pounds spent on child care and the extra clothing one must have for the job. The heavier costs to working mothers are, we think, worry about the hours their children may spend in inadequate care and anxiety about whether the children are happy and whether they are being good parents.

We do not need psychology to justify mothers' employment. Mothers, like other people, work for a variety of reasons, from economic need to personal fulfilment. The former is far more often the reason than the latter, as was discussed in Chapter 2. Frequency does not make economic reasons more legitimate than psychological reasons for working.

The results of psychological research *can*, however, help mothers to feel more comfortable with their choices about work and child care, and in this chapter we look at the relationships between children and parents in different kinds of families – traditional and non-traditional – and at the effects of divorce and single parenthood on children and their parents. The studies raise the issue of why working mothers should feel guilty. As a start, this guilt of working mothers raises an important question: Why don't fathers feel guilty about working?

The Rediscovery of Fathers as Parents

It was inevitable. As mothers of young children went to work and the women's movement began to make headway against legal and emotional barriers to equal rights, the inevitable question was raised: where have fathers been? The answer is, they've been hiding out on the job for 200 years. When work and home were separated by the Industrial Revolution, fathers withdrew from the household to work long hours at the factory, mine or office. In the growing middle classes, after the Napoleonic Wars, husband and wife ceased working together in the house because men needed to leave home in order to earn money. Thus although many fathers were intensely interested in their children, delighted by their achievements and desperately concerned when they were ill, they were far less closely involved in their children's care.

The same economic and social forces that kept women out of the work force excluded fathers from child rearing. The psychological justification for the segregation of women in the home and men in the workplace was that mothers were special caregivers, and by implication fathers were not fit parents. At least, fathers were reputed to be unable to give young children the emotional support and intimacy that mothers could. Just as mothers were captives in the home, fathers were hostages in the workplace. Women were not allowed to be economically competent; men were not permitted to be emotionally competent. They were primarily distant figures – either potential disciplinarians or rewarders of the good. In contrast, William Cobbett – who raised his own children, worked at home in order to do so, and wrote *Advice to Young Men and Incidentally Young Women . . . On How to be a Father* in 1829 – was very much an eccentric, an exceptional figure.

John Nash (1976), a historian of the family, sees a gradual change in fathers' domestic roles from the nineteenth to mid-twentieth centuries in both Europe and America. From early colonial times in North America to the mid twentieth century, the stern and distant father was the ideal. He was the unemotional model of dignity and honour. He was above sentimentality and mere children. The Protestant ethic called for the father to devote himself to and show his Godliness through good economic works.

> [T]he man of the house worked hard to support the family, and his role as supporter excused him from direct concern with domestic affairs. Indeed he was almost expected to absent himself from the family to perform this duty. In rural communities interaction with sons began only when they were old

enough to join the father in his labours. In most instances, fathers saw little of their daughters, who spent their time with the mother.

In urban groups, as the Industrial Revolution reached North America, the same ethic kept the father at the factory or office for long hours, and no domestic duties were expected of him. The same ethic also appeared in Europe (Nash, 1976, p. 74).

In the nineteenth and early twentieth centuries the concern and affection that fathers felt for their children is evident from their letters, autobiographies and diaries (Pollock, 1983). They even wrote to parents' magazines: the increasing numbers of fathers who wrote to Ada Ballin of *Baby* magazine, at the end of the nineteenth century, led her to rename her 'Mothers' Parliament' 'Parents' Parliament'. The Child Study Movement, as we've seen, sanctioned fathers in the nursery as scientific observers of their children. But they were relatively rarely involved in the children's care. Watson in the 1920s allotted fathers half an hour with their children: 'It keeps the children used to male society. They have a chance to ply him with questions' (impossible, of course, for their mother to answer questions . . .).

The ethic of distant father and the home-bound mother prevailed until millions of women joined the labour force at the start of the Second World War. With the cessation of hostilities, the employment of many of these millions also ended. A new kind of hostility began when many women were forced out of jobs and back into the kitchen.

The Second World War: two revolutions

The Second World War brought two major changes in mothering and child care. A permanent revolution in birthing practices arose from the blitz in London. Mothers with newborn babies had to be moved to the safety of the underground every evening to avoid the nightly German bombings. The only way for maternity patients to get to the shelters was by walking and carrying their own babies. So the babies had to be close at hand.

Surprisingly, mothers had fewer medical problems after birth when they got up and moved around soon after delivery than when they stayed in bed. Instead of emerging from confinement as semi-invalids after being bedridden for two weeks, those who got out of bed within a day stayed strong and healthy. The blitz had one happy outcome. The revolution in birthing practice was retained for sound economic reasons. It is much cheaper to keep new mothers in the hospital for only three days than for two weeks and to keep healthy newborn babies with their mothers, rather than in a special nursery.

A temporary revolution was the national approval of the employment of mothers with young children, as we saw in Chapter 2. It was the patriotic duty of every able-bodied person to aid in the war effort. Many men were away from their jobs, fighting, and there were not enough men left at home to fill in. The only solution was to send women out of the home and into the factories and offices. A suddenly nonsexist country urged women to become workers on the land and in the factories.

Because women were badly needed, the government and industries also provided day nurseries for the children. Pre-school children by the tens of thousands were put into day nurseries. The social literature of the day is silent on any *bad* effects of the day care.

It is strange how in wartime mothers can go to work without endangering their young children's psyches, but when they are not required in the labour force their employment becomes a hazard to children's mental health. Psychoanalysts in Britain were concerned about the dangers to children of separation from their mothers during the war, but this concern was primarily focused upon the consequences of evacuation, rather than the dangers of day nurseries. Bowlby wrote in 1940, drawing on his earlier work with juvenile thieves, rather than study of evacuation *per se*, that

> the prolonged separation of small children from their homes is one of the outstanding causes of the development of a criminal character. No scheme for the evacuation of young children which ignores this fact should be considered (Bowlby, 1940a, p. 190).

Interestingly, in 1940 Bowlby did not see daily separations from the mother as necessarily having damaging consequences. He saw poor mothering as the root of neuroses, but considered full-time mothers just as dangerous in this respect as those who were working.

Provided breaks are not too long, and continuity is preserved, there seems no evidence to suppose that the child who is always with his mother is any better off than the child who only sees her for a few hours a day, and not at all for odd holiday weeks (Bowlby, 1940b, p. 177).

From the short war to the long war

The Second World War lasted six years. The war of the sexes over justice and equality is the longest war in history (Tavris and Wade, 1984). The former is no match for the latter in importance to the roles of mothers, fathers and the legitimacy of child care.

The 1950s were a solid, reproductive era. In the years after the war, when millions of men returned home, families reproduced at an unprecedented rate. Fathers joined the grey-flannel crowd, children roamed new suburban neighbourhoods, and their mothers kept house. Fathers did not yet expect to share domestic chores or child care. Mothers did not expect to be employed. It was a pretty solid arrangement.

Family stability was eroding, however. The divorce rate soared. Illegitimacy became a topic of polite conversation in even the best families. Sexual licence was given, it seemed, to every teenager as a birthright. Extra-marital affairs (which used to be called adultery) served as a humorous theme for plays, novels, and films. The solid family that was intent on reproduction and respectability was breaking apart. One could say, however, that nontraditional families were evolving.

As many women were soon to discover, the protections of marriage and motherhood were going to buy them about as much as that apple pie they baked every Thursday. The economic realities of divorce and single parenthood crashed on many bouffant heads.

A solution to the vulnerability of mothers was to become economically and personally more independent. It is not enough to know how to do a job. One also needs the courage to get up in the morning, get out of the house and do the job. One needs the confidence to defend oneself in the marketplace and to weather inevitable setbacks. That is personal independence, a precious commodity that many women found in short supply after fifteen years at home.

The companion solution to the greater independence of mothers was to engage fathers in the rearing of their children. While mothers went to work to hone their economic and personal skills, fathers could afford to devote some of themselves and their time to the children – not to mention the vacuuming, shopping and washing up. Some fathers volunteered to become more active parents; others were pushed into the role by the example of other fathers and by wives who insisted on more equality. Most men dallied at housework, but they did begin to spend more time with their children. And so it was, in brief, that some fathers came to be real parents to their young children.

Child care is embarrassing

For such fathers, the 1950s were an awkward era. These fathers were beginning to try new ways of being. Their own fathers had rarely tried the roles they themselves had to attempt. Fathers were actually beginning to take a share of child care, but they were not comfortable about it. From the 1950s until the mid 1960s, fathers were tentative parents.

Through much of this period, fathers who helped with child care were ridiculed as henpecked and unmasculine. Cartoons and films before about 1960 portrayed fathers' care of young children as embarrassing, inappropriate and inept. Wrapped in mother's ruffled apron, father was shown aiming spoonfuls of cereal at a reluctant baby. The baby was coated from crown to rump with the gooey mess. In one film, the climactic scene shows baby dumping the bowl over Dad's head. As the cereal trickles down poor father's cheeks, the audience roars. Fathers' alleged inability to learn the art of changing nappies provided equally comic relief in several films of the 1940s and 1950s. Combine a wriggling ten-month-old and a bumbling father with nappy pins in his mouth in a hopeless struggle to wrap the baby's bottom, and you had a hilarious scene. Fathers were shown as uncomfortable in the care of their young, and most of all embarrassed that someone might think this was their usual role.

Father as a parent

Gradually psychologists and other experts sniffed the winds of cultural change and reappraised fathers' roles. Beginning in the early 1950s, books and articles began to appear with titles such as *Fathers are Parents too* (English and Foster, 1953) and *It's Time Father got Back into the Family* (Nash, 1956). At first, interest was limited to a few fringe psychologists and fathers. Those baby books that had sections on 'Father' discussed him chiefly as a problem – is he too effeminate? Jealous? Too often absent? (Hardyment, 1984, p. 232). Later, with the flowering of the women's movement, fathers became an 'in' item. But as late as 1965 fathers' care is still presented in terms of *special*, different activities with children. In Phyllis Hostler's *Child's World* the advice is that when children are older

> father and child can go off alone on expeditions that only daddies can deal with competently, visits to the science museum, the railway station, or the new building site.

From the 1950s to the 1970s, psychologists were happy to follow the cultural current and to rediscover father as a parent. Still, he could not be just another parent in the old maternal style. To be just like mother would make father redundant. So the research questions focused on father's unique contribution to children's development.

Study after study asked how father's influences were *different* from mother's. What can father do that mother cannot? The most obvious difference between parents is sex. Surely the fact that one parent is a man and one a woman must have something to do with boys being boys, and girls being girls. Other facts about parents, such as intelligence and personality, which both have to offer to their children, were ignored. It was children's sex roles – learning to be masculine and feminine – that dominated researchers' interests. If father had a unique role in the family, it probably had to do with sex. And if father was to return to child care, he had to have a special role.

As the new era of fathers-as-parents dawned, the experts discovered that many children did not have 'real' fathers in the home, because of divorce, illegitimacy, death and foreign wars. This was especially true of minority and lower-class families. Fathers re-entered the family and psychological consciousness as the parent who might not be at home after all. So the principal question became, 'What's *wrong* with children when their father is absent?' If fathers are important to children's psychological development, then their absence should have bad effects.

It is ironic that psychologists and other experts first recognized father as an important parent by mourning his frequent loss. After all, the culture had excluded him as a psychological parent for two centuries.

The late 1950s to early 1970s saw many studies of femininity and masculinity in boys whose fathers were present or absent in their lives. (No one worried much about the girls yet.) Boys whose fathers were absent in the pre-school period turned out to be less stereotypically masculine than boys whose fathers left home in their school years or boys with fathers at home. Because of the prevailing cultural stereotype of masculinity and feminity, that boys without fathers in the pre-school period were less 'masculine' was thought to be unfortunate (Belsky, Lerner and Spanier, 1984).

Note that practically no one asked about how fathers actually interact with their children, or about fathers' relationships with their children. Few thought that family patterns, such as a father's absence, could have different meaning in different cultures.

No one asked whether the two-parent, two-child family was the ideal for child rearing; it was simply assumed to be. And the parents had to be married. The only man who was fit to have an influence on children – a good influence, that is – was the father of the child who was also the husband of the child's mother. No one suggested that marriage was not the only way to get a man into a child's life. No one had noticed that in black communities in the US, for instance, other males – such as uncles, grandfathers, mother's lovers, and older brothers – often play important roles in young children's lives. And no one said anything about the fact that children with and without fathers in the home were more alike than different. Researchers and policy makers were intent on finding out what is wrong with children in mother-headed households. In 1969, Daniel Patrick Moynihan attributed the social, economic and educational problems of black Americans to the high rate of single parenthood among blacks. In one masterful sweep, Moynihan obliterated cultural differences and poverty from our consciousness by focusing our attentions on the evils of father absence.

Not until the late 1970s did psychologists begin to recognize the diverse family patterns that can be good for children. No one kind of family is necessarily good, but all can work to rear children well. Other factors, such as the kinds of relationships people in the family have with each other and the kinds of interactions adults have with the children, are more important than the biological or legal connections of family members.

What Fathers Can Do for Children

Mothers wipe babies' noses, fathers toss them in the air. Mothers change toddlers' nappies, fathers play hide-and-seek with them in the living room (Parke, 1981). Even if this picture seems stereotyped – and it is – the social sciences have advanced their view over that of twenty years ago. Both fathers' behaviour and our attitude towards it has changed.

Many fathers now have discovered that men can be just as loving parents to babies – from birth – and to young children as women can. And psychologists are beginning to catch up with them, and to document that unlike the old style distant parent, fathers now play with their children and give them joy.

According to current psychologists' views of mothers and fathers, both are important people in their young childrens' lives, but they serve somewhat different purposes. Both parents are attachment figures who can make the baby feel secure, even before it is a year old. But fathers are often more fun to play with (Lamb, 1975). Babies are more likely to go to their mothers if they are distressed, because the mother is more often the comforting person. Many fathers also serve this purpose, and most babies are happy enough to have their wounds bound by daddy, if mummy is not there. Other adults can also comfort babies. It's just that, given a choice, more babies prefer their mother.

By the time they are two years old, many boys prefer the company of their fathers, who play rough-and-tumble games. Girls are equally happy with either parent. The fact that fathers are more likely to play is because in most households mothers still have the major responsibilities for physical care. Feeding, cleaning and training young children are not typical responsibilities in the carefree roles that many fathers have (Lamb, 1975; Parke and Sawin, 1980; Parke, 1981).

Yet mothers and fathers tend to act in similar ways towards their young children. Psychologists are still highlighting small differences rather than the overwhelming similarities in parents' behaviour. This is probably a hangover from the 1950s re-emergence of the father as a parent. He has to be special. The best summary of the evidence on mothers and fathers with their babies is that young children of both sexes, in most circumstances, like both parents equally well. Fathers, like mothers, are good parents first and gender representatives second.

In the 1980s fathers have become real people. Men were always real people – often bigger than life – but fathers in earlier decades of this century were often shadowy figures, lurking on the periphery of the family circle. Now fathers have joined the family circle as important parents in their own right. And it's not a moment too soon. Since mothers have gone to work in unprecedented numbers, someone has to keep the circle whole.

More and more families depend on fathers for a significant part of child-care responsibilities, both direct and indirect. The OPCS National Survey of 1980 reports that 59 per cent of working mothers saw their husbands as sharing child care half-and-half with them – note that this means that around 40 per cent of working mothers are doing most or all of the work of child care in addition to their jobs outside the home. The actual child care taken on by fathers and mothers according to this survey differed just as it did in the detailed psychological studies that we described above: mothers did most of the routine physical work, fathers played with the children and took them out. Housework is another story: husbands were less likely to help with the housework than with the children. The burden on working mothers is still great, especially for those who work full time (Martin and Roberts, 1984). But it does appear that fathers are increasingly involved in the actual care of their babies, and they are also more involved in the planning of child care when their wives work. We can only applaud, and wish the next generation of fathers more pleasure in sharing than many of our generation enjoyed.

Families Come in Many Forms

Families take many forms. A family is not a heterosexual couple with 2.2 children and a neat garden. From a child-development perspective, a family is most usefully defined as a system in which children grow up. The family group can be made up of a married couple and their children, but it can also be made up of a mother and her children, a father and his children, grandparents and grandchildren, assorted other relatives, friends, and even several unmarried people who are rearing children.

By other definitions, a family is an economic unit that does not have to include children at all. To economists, a family unit is a group of related persons whose resources are shared. Many economic families do function to rear children, but the elderly, the childless couple, and roommates are also economic family units.

It is important for practical and psychological reasons to call any reasonably stable group that rears children a family. Someone has to provide housing, food, schooling, medical and dental care, and be responsible for children. Whatever the composition of the adult group, from a legal point of view it is generally recognized by school and other authorities as the child's family. The advantage of this view is that traditional and nontraditional families can all be seen to serve the interests of children. Children can also feel comfortable with an approved family form, even if it is not traditional.

All family forms have strengths and weaknesses. The typical assets of the two-parent model are not the same as those of the one-parent, step-parent or grandparent variety, although there is virtually no psychological research on families other than the two-parent model. Only recently have some studies begun to focus on nontraditional families.

With the striking demographic changes of the last decades, psychologists are beginning to look at single parents and divorced families. Sandra Scarr worked on a group of families of young children (Scarr, 1983) that included 125 single- and two-parent families. The children's development did not depend on having both parents living in the household. Rather, children with higher intellectual levels, greater emotional stability, and better personal adjustment came from families with more intelligent mothers who handled their two- to four-year-olds in more benign ways. Mothers whose children developed well were more likely to talk to their children, reason with them and explain difficulties to them, rather than hit them. Whether the father lived in the household or not was irrelevant to the child's development. In fact, many fathers who did not reside with the mother had a continuing relationship with her and the child.

This study was located in a community where the vast majority of the mothers work and the children are in some form of day care. Community attitudes favour, or at least condone, maternal employment. Single mothers are frowned upon slightly but not severely. It is important to recognize that all cultural groups have their own standards of what constitutes a proper family. The assets and liabilities of different family forms vary with the approval or disapproval afforded them by the community. In fact, much of what families can do for children depends on the *meaning* that the community gives to their family form, not on what they can actually do for children. If the community undercuts and criticizes single-parent families, for example, both the parents and their children may feel disadvantaged, even if they are functioning quite well.

No family form is best at meeting all problems at all times in children's lives. Traditional families typically provide good control over children but have a hard time letting go. Single parents often expect a great deal of independence from their children, which can be hard on young children but good for older ones. Regardless of the family form, the care that is appropriate for children changes as they mature. Limits on children's behaviour must change; parental controls must change. Older children need less physical care and a more sophisticated kind of psychological care than younger children. All children need limits on their behaviour that are appropriate to their own developmental status. Two-year-olds cannot be trusted to decide whether to cross the street, but ten-year-olds generally can. Teenagers need parental guidance on future goals and limits on what they do with their friends, but they do not want to be told what to wear, eat or hear. They need more time to themselves and more space to try out their own ways of doing and being. Eventually, as they reach adulthood, children need greater freedom from parental involvement in the details of their daily lives or else they will not be permitted to become independent human adults.

Few psychologists have approached the study of families with an eye to the possible strengths and weaknesses of different constellations of adults in the rearing of children. Commitment to the two-parent nuclear family has led us to discount the possible strengths of other types. In the next sections, we bring together results from the research literature and speculate on the effects of traditional and nontraditional families. We recognize that individual families are as different as individual people and that it is very risky to generalize from the average of a group to any one person's situation. We think it is possible, however, to describe the characteristic problems of several types of families and to show that all can do a good job of rearing children.

Traditional Families

In the traditional family, most mothers and fathers have their own distinct tasks. Fathers have different relationships with their young children than mothers do. Mothers traditionally take care of children by feeding, clothing, cleaning and giving affection. Fathers traditionally earn money outside the home and while at home play and talk with their children. Fathers in such families do less physical work for the youngsters, are less demonstrative but more entertaining than mothers.

Fathers in traditional families also spend far less time with young children than mothers do. Because fathers are sometimes less affectionate as well, the children are often more strongly attached to mother as their source of security. Fathers can feel left out and unimportant. Even though contemporary traditional fathers spend more time with their children than Victorian fathers did, there is still more distance in the father-child relationship than is necessary or even most rewarding for fathers. The rewards of parenthood are less available to distant fathers.

Many mothers in traditional families thrive on their children's dependence. Because their primary role is child care, traditional mothers need to be needed. Their role is to serve the family. Clearly, young children need caring, attentive adults. Traditional mothers often fill this role well, and young children meet their needs well. But many mothers today are not entirely comfortable with this role. More than half the mothers of pre-school children have got jobs, and when asked if they would prefer to be at home full time, the majority say no. What used to be an expected and rewarded devotion to full-time child rearing is now less respected. The phrase 'just a housewife' became a self-derogation of the 1970s. In our view, it's a shame if mothers do not have the choice, within their economic means, to decide how much time to devote to parenting and how much to employment. Any loss of options should be regretted. Some women want to stay at home until their children are at school or are at a later stage of greater independence. This should be a possible and rewarded choice. Others will make other choices, and they too should have comfortable options. It is true that the present generation of women have had to push for employment opportunities and scramble for child care, but in pressing for their opportunities we must not lose sight of the value of a family pattern that can be a very happy world for mothers and for children.

More difficulties arise with older children. Mothers who have been full-time housewives during the time that their children are under eighteen years old often find it difficult to manage the transition to their children's adolescence – even more difficult than working mothers – because a traditional mother's role is primarily in child care. The nonemployed mother is eased out of her major role by her children's increasing need for independence. For some mothers, the transition to not being needed is painful: Mum stays at home just to be there when her twelve-year-old comes home from school, only to find him shouting 'Hi, Mum,' grabbing two apples, and running out of the door to meet his friends for soccer. He can make his own tea and prefers to do so. And he prefers his own friends' company to his mother's in the late afternoon. So Mum is left, busying herself with making dinner and waiting for her husband to come home.

When the nest is empty

For many a mother who doesn't work, the 'empty nest' looms like a black hole. Her children have grown too old to need her full-time care. What used to be appropriate attention to little ones turns into unwarranted intrusiveness in the lives of older children, who flee the home to gain some independence. Children's growing up presents adjustment problems for most mothers, but especially for the mother who has not worked. As Chapter 6 will describe, remarkable changes in independence and competence to manage one's own affairs occur even between two and five years. Add another ten years to the child's maturity, and you have a partially empty nest.

Some mothers weep when their children go to nursery school, lament the day they start having dinner at school, and go into mourning when a child leaves for university. They are tempted to call the child at college just 'to make sure everything is all right'. Such mothers need the adolescent to need them, but unfortunately for them the child is no longer the adorable pre-school child who thrived on Mum's devoted attention. If the child is a healthy young person, she wants to determine when she needs to talk to Mum, which is unlikely to be as often as many mothers would like. When the children grow up, the mother has lost her role. She's a robin without an egg to sit on.

Mothers who haven't worked often turn to their husbands for satisfactions when the children are grown. For some couples, this can be the most satisfying period of their lives. They can devote to each other the loving attention that was previously focused on the children. Other couples find each other intolerable when their mutual interest in the children no longer serves as a bond between them. Many couples now seek divorces after twenty to thirty years of marriage, when the last child has left home.

The hours per day that mothers are needed for direct child care diminish rapidly as children get older, yet even older children need after-school supervision. Mothers who do not work are at home to provide the indirect care needed, but it fills only a few minutes of their life. Some communities, and some other industrialized nations, provide supervised after-school sports and recreation for all their older children and youths, so that mothers are not left home waiting for a non-event.

Mothering changes. Many mothers of ten- to twenty-year-olds substitute a broader form of indirect child rearing for direct child care when their children no longer need their constant attention. Community service to schools, libraries, hospitals, and other social service agencies is a traditional form of extended mothering, if you will. Nonemployed mothers of older children involve themselves in helping with school outings and arranging school jumble sales. In these ways they are still involved in child rearing but they are not dependent on their children's company at the end of the school day. Community groups rely on volunteer mothers' valuable services, contributions that have declined rapidly as more mothers have taken jobs. Schools, churches and other groups now depend far more on cash to purchase goods and services than they did a decade ago, when mothers filled their lives with beneficial contributions of their extended mothering.

Another way to avoid the bleak future of the empty nest is to build into one's life other satisfactions, aspirations, and possibilities. Whether mother or father, traditional male and female roles are limiting. Traditional parents have difficulty with changes in their lives, because their roles are defined by gender. 'Real' men do not take care of babies or cook meals. 'Real' women do not mend cars or bring home the wages. People with such attitudes seem to be prejudicing the contemporary gods against them. In the event of divorce, both parents, and their children, are vulnerable.

The effects of divorce

Divorce raises harsh personal issues for a mother who has no job, especially if she not only loses her traditional husband but is forced to go to work. She has not worked outside the home for several years. Does she still have skills that employers need? Can she manage a schedule of working at the job and caring for her children and home? What will become of the children, now deserted by an absent father and an employed mother? Who will invite her to dinner? All of her social life was through her husband. A mother who has devoted herself to the exclusive job of rearing children is less prepared to deal with the emotional, social and economic aftermath of divorce than women whose roles have been more diverse. Divorce runs over the traditional mother like a double-decker bus; the less traditional woman is merely flattened by a VW.

During the first year after divorce, mothers who have not been employed feel especially incompetent as mothers and as women. They are typically depressed and their households are chaotic. Mavis Hetherington and her colleagues studied seventy-two newly divorced couples with pre-school children and compared the parents' and children's functioning with a similar number of intact families. The study traced changes in the family members over two years after the divorce. They found that divorce is stressful for most parents and their children, of course, but some parents were especially vulnerable to the dissolution of the marriage. Previously unemployed mothers fared worst when they had to go to work at the time of the divorce. Mothers gained self-esteem and feelings of competence from their new jobs, but the children got out of hand. Discipline flagged, and the children's behaviour worsened.

> Maternal employment was an example of a situation that had a positive outcome for mothers but not necessarily for children. If the mother had always worked or did not begin work until about two years after the divorce, there appeared to be no deleterious effects on the (pre-school) children. If mothers began work around the time of separation and divorce, this was associated with a high incidence of behaviour problems in children, especially in boys. It was as though the children had gone through a double loss of the mother and the father, which compounded their stress (Hetherington, Cox and Cox, 1982, pp. 248–9).

'Traditional' mothers whose home has been broken and who have to leave young children for employment suffer enormous disruption in their lives. So do the children, who are not used to having other caregivers or being out of their homes for most of the day. Hetherington found that the children of newly employed mothers are especially disobedient and disturbed, although most of the divorced families experience disturbances in both parenting and child behaviour. The children of divorced parents are more dependent, play in a less sustained fashion in the nursery school, and are difficult to manage at home.

The divorced mother is likely to be harassed by her children, particularly her sons. In the first year after divorce, they do not obey or attend to her and, in fact, are not very friendly. They nag and whine, demand attention, and ignore her attempts to control them. Sons are more aggressive in divorced families, even two years after the divorce.

> Some divorced mothers described their relationship with their child as 'declared war', a 'struggle for survival', 'the old Chinese water torture', or 'like getting bitten to death by ducks' (Hetherington, Cox, and Cox, 1982, p. 258).

After the first year, however, the typical divorced mother has pulled herself together, regained control of the kids, and adjusted to her new role as employee and mother. The daughters have settled down and regained their good behaviour and the sons are improving. But the first year is hell (Hetherington, Cox and Cox, 1982).

Interestingly enough, fathers who do not have custody of children and who have lived in traditional families are even more disabled in the first year after divorce than mothers. Not only have they lost significant amounts of contact with their children, but many cannot boil water, let alone fix an appetizing meal. The vacuum cleaner is a stranger invention than the microcomputer. Left on their own to cope, many traditional fathers founder. Such fathers are more depressed a year after the divorce than mothers who are left with the children (Hetherington, Cox and Cox, 1982). It is true that divorced fathers often 'live it up', have more money to spend than their divorced spouses, and treat the children to Christmas every other weekend. But it is also true that their lives are emptier, lonelier and more disrupted than those of mothers who have the children to care for. But fathers fight their way back to mental health sooner than mothers. Two years after divorce, fathers have made better adjustments, in part because they have more adult companionship and social activities than do divorced mothers.

John Santrock and his colleagues studied divorced families in which fathers have custody of their children, compared with mother-custody families (Santrock, Warshak and Elliott, in Lamb, 1982, pp. 289–314). One interesting contrast between the two types of divorced families is that fathers with child custody make greater use of child-care help from day-care centres, child-care homes, and babysitters than mothers with custody (twenty-four hours per week versus eleven hours per week). Fathers often have more money and can afford more child care. But the good effects of child care were evident in father- and mother-headed families. In both kinds of families, 'total contact with adult caretakers was positively related to the child's warmth, sociability and social conformity as observed in the laboratory' (p. 294). Children with more contact with parents and other adults fare better than children with fewer adult contacts, even if they have a lot of contact with one parent. Children can actually gain some stability and protection from the inevitable parental upsets that arise from divorce by having relationships with other adults who are not so stressed.

This summary of the divorce literature concludes that traditional families, in which a mother stays home full time and a father has little responsibility for children or house work, have a more difficult time coping with divorce than less traditional families. If a mother is already employed, if the children are used to being looked after by someone else and their father knows how to make spaghetti, both parents and children suffer less from divorce. We are not advocating defensive living, like defensive driving, to avert an accident. There is something to be said, however, for anticipating possible dangers. Having both housewifely skills and employment is rather like wearing your seatbelt: in case of accident, you are less likely to be seriously injured. We have accepted the good sense of our seatbelt law; there is a parallel case to be made for protecting children in case of divorce.

Nontraditional Families

The 1960s and 1970s saw an outpouring of expert advice and research on the 'tragedy' of divorce, the inadequacies of single-parent families, the menace of working mothers, and the disaster of teenage pregnancy. Debates over the right of homosexual couples to rear children and the advisability of joint custody in divorce cases occupied thousands of magazine pages and everyone's mental space. TV shows, newspapers and women's magazines devoted millions of words to allegedly disastrous changes in The Family. Changes in family forms can be a social problem, but not always because they are bad for children. Sometimes they are just upsetting to adults. Alternative family forms were a greater threat to entrenched values than to children.

Some groups within our society have had a larger percentage of nontraditional families – single, divorced and separated mothers, grandparent families, and care by other relatives – than the majority of the community. Black mothers have often worked to support their children. The employment of other mothers is catching up. Nontraditional forms of families in the white community began to be noticed as the divorce and illegitimacy rates soared in the 1960s. Suddenly, Sally Brown down the street was an unwed mother who kept her baby, and the McNamaras were getting a divorce. Mrs McNamara had to go to work, and she had trouble finding care for her two pre-school children. Her parents lived 200 miles away, and her sister nearly as far. No officially organized care existed in her town, so she paid an elderly lady down the street and prayed that the children would not drive her crazy. The solid, traditional two-parent family of the 1950s seemed about to become an endangered species. Many people began to notice that there were few community resources to help single and divorced parents to care for their children while they had to work. But national attention was focused on lamenting the evils of single parenthood and divorce rather than on what kinds of support would help such families to function better.

Single-parent families

In the 1980s it may seem like ancient history to describe the horror with which nontraditional families were treated, but their emergence among the solid middle class created a revolution in thinking about The Family. Note the use of the singular term *Family*, as though there ever were only one form, as though children had never before lived with single mothers or grandparents. How about maiden Aunt Maude, who in the 1920s reared her dead sister's children? It was, of course, the ideal family that had two parents, two children, a garage and a tidy garden.

Single parenthood has been blamed for many ills that belong more properly to poverty and to our lack of community and family resources. Studies of single-parent households necessarily confuse low income, low educational levels, minority group membership, and a host of other disadvantages with single parenthood. Findings that children from single-parent families do not perform as well in school as children from two-parent homes could probably just as well be attributed to these other factors as to living with only one parent.

We don't yet know what the effects of growing up in a single-parent family are likely to be in Britain – psychologists haven't yet asked the right kinds of questions. For example, one can imagine that a mature, intelligent single mother without the distractions of a husband might actually give more attention to her children. On the other hand, the stresses with which a single mother has to cope may all too often prove overwhelming.

Let us consider whether research from other countries suggests that the single-parent family is the disaster psychologists and other experts claimed in previous decades. What changed in the 1980s was the willingness of experts to consider that some other family forms might actually do a decent job of rearing children. With the great increase in the number of divorced and other single-parent families, it is not surprising that in the 1980s studies from America are beginning to be published on the child-rearing strengths of non-traditional families.

In a new study of traditional and nontraditional families, a group of Californian investigators (Eiduson *et al.*, 1982) studied fifty single-mother families, fifty unmarried families with a 'social contract' relationship, fifty communal-living families, and fifty traditional two-parent families. The families entered the study in the last trimester of pregnancy and continued until the child was four years old. As you may imagine in such a set of families, there were vast differences in parental values, many differences in material and cultural life-style, and different kinds of relationships with extended family and others. Communal-living parents were more likely to share the baby's care with other adults in the group, and the mothers were more likely to breast-feed than mothers in traditional families. Traditional couples had more money and more material possessions than any other group and were less likely to share child care with others. Naturally, some families in each group functioned particularly well, while others did not – the same range of individual differences one finds in any study of families, traditional or not.

One might expect that communal families would have a far more casual approach to the child's daily routine of eating and sleeping and to issues such as toilet training. The stereotype of the traditional family with a full-time mother at home is of a rigorously kept daily routine of meals on time, a lot of educational interactions between mother and child, a sparkling clean kitchen, and no ring-around-the-collar. In single-parent households, one might predict some neglect of the child by an overburdened mother. The results of the study are surprising, therefore. Overall, there were no differences among the groups in how well they functioned as parents.

There were fewer differences in practice than in philosophy. Observations of parents' interactions with their young children at home indicated some differences but many more similarities. The common features of daily life for the child were those details of child care that would be observed almost anywhere in the world. Children were fed on a regular basis, put to bed, played with, and taken for trips to the local shops and the doctor. Even in discipline and in scheduled activities, where one would expect great differences between traditional and nontraditional parents, the differences in actual practice were small compared to the individual differences within each kind of family.

The most important finding, however, is that there were no differences in the children's development in infancy or early childhood. In the first year of life, the children in the four kinds of families had the same varieties of mental and physical development and the same kinds of attachments to their parents. At three years old the children in the four groups did not differ on average in intelligence, creativity, aggressiveness, security of attachment to parents, activity level, tolerance for frustration, social competence, emotional adjustment, or maturity. Despite many deep and pervasive differences among the families in child-rearing philosophy, there were *no* differences in the children's development.

> In sum, the psychological development of the children was assessed thoroughly and repeatedly during the first three years of their lives. Although a number of developmental constructs were assessed, the life-style of the family in which the children were being raised has no systematic effect on the children's development. Stated differently, the children in all groups appeared to be developing normally (Eiduson *et al.*, 1982, p. 344).

The punch line from this important study is that children thrive in a variety of family forms, that they develop normally with single parents, with unmarried parents, with multiple caretakers in a communal setting, and with traditional two-parent families. What children require is loving and attentive adults, not a particular family type.

Fathers as primary caregivers

In the 1980s some fathers became more involved in the care of their children in nontraditional ways, such as keeping the children while their wives worked. These families have reversed the roles; mother works while father cares for the child. Can fathers be as good at the nitty-gritty of child care and in the emotional support of babies and young children as mothers are? Traditional psychology, whether Freudian or Watsonian, would predict disaster. In the 1980s, however, the cultural views of one highly educated group of young parents have made nontraditional fathers the heroes of the era.

In a series of studies in the United States (Radin, 1982), Australia (Russell, 1982), Israel (Sagi, 1982) and the Netherlands (Lamb *et al.*, 1982), investigators report some beneficial results of fathers' involvement as primary or equal caregivers for their children. In some families the father was the one who stayed at home; in others, husband and wife shared equally in child care, taking over for each other while each worked or studied. Fathers with primary or equal responsibility for the child manage the child's routine and the household in much the same ways that mothers do. Not surprisingly for men who are willing to assume primary child-care responsibilities, they get meals, do the washing, shop, watch TV, talk and play with the child. In other words, for whichever parent is at home with responsibility for the child and the household, the task demands evoke most of the same behaviour.

Investigators of these nontraditional families conclude that the children are actually at an advantage compared with others reared in more traditional families. Children with caregiving fathers are found to have slightly better intellectual skills than others with caregiving mothers in traditional families. We doubt the legitimacy of this claim, because those who choose such arrangements are typically bright and highly educated parents who would have bright children whichever parent stayed home or whatever good care they chose in other settings. There were no differences in emotional or social development, which at least testifies to the fact that fathers are not an emotional disaster.

Investigators of nontraditional families express enthusiasm for their qualities as child-rearing environments for children. In describing one such study of nontraditional families in which the fathers were heavily involved in child rearing, an American psychologist, Norma Radin, found that fathers' high involvement was associated with greater cognitive enrichment in the home by both parents and lesser parental punitiveness toward the child. Again, both these factors are associated in our own research primarily with higher parental intelligence and not with fathers' caregiving *per se*. Nonetheless, Radin reports that father caregiving is a compatible and good arrangement for some parents.

> Once such an arrangement gets under way, and the fathers are satisfied with the exchange, the fathers, who have maintained their masculine identity, appear to increase their efforts to stimulate their children's cognitive growth, particularly their daughters', and become involved in direct teaching of their sons; the mothers, still feminine in orientation, reduce such activities. With their sexual identities unaffected, the children's internality (self-direction) and intellectual abilities appear to flourish. As a whole, the evidence should not discourage other families from considering this alternative family style (Radin, 1982, pp. 201–202).

One does not have to accept Norma Radin's enthusiasm about 'new wave' families to see that alternate family forms may be perfectly capable of providing good care for children. Again, we have evidence that children thrive under conditions where they get loving interaction with familiar adults, who do not have to be only their biological mothers.

The adjustments of working mothers

Finally, being employed may be good for a mother's mental health and that of her family. Believe it or not, working mothers who like their jobs have better personal adjustments, are happier, and are less depressed than full-time mothers, even those who prefer being at home with their children. Divorced mothers with jobs are especially better off than divorced mothers without jobs (Hetherington, Cox and Cox, 1982). Colleagues at work can soothe the worst effects of the emotional trauma of divorce.

The worst adjusted and the most unhappy women are mothers at home who wish they could be employed (Crosby, 1982). Non-employed mothers who wish they could get out of the house to a workplace are the most frustrated and depressed mothers in samples of women in several studies. They feel trapped and lonely, lack self-confidence, and appear disorganized.

Depressed mothers have depressing effects on their children. Children of depressed mothers avoid them and shun attention from other adults. The children seem to develop an avoidance of emotional involvements with others when their mothers are depressed (Kellam *et al.*, 1983).

As pre-school children they have more behaviour problems and are more difficult. The emotional adjustment of mothers to their roles has a real impact on their children.

To sum up, if you can manage the logistical and psychological hurdles with which we began this chapter, on balance we believe that working and enjoying your job is probably good for you and for your family, whatever kind of family you live in.

PART THREE

What Children Need

CHAPTER SIX

The Nature of Babies and Pre-school Children

Tommy sits on the floor banging his blocks together, enjoying the noise. Mother is nearby setting the table for lunch. The doorbell rings and in comes Granny who hasn't seen her only grandchild for four months. On her last visit, he was just barely sitting up, and now he's ten months old. What a joy to hold him again! As Granny approaches, Tommy's bottom lip quivers, he turns his head toward the wall, and begins to whimper. As she stoops to sweep him into her arms, he screams in distress. One would think he was being attacked by a hungry wolf. Mother is very embarrassed and confused. Why is her ordinarily friendly baby reacting this way to his Granny?

Jessica's second birthday party is in full swing. Four other children are strewing the living room with new toys. Disputes break out. They are not arguments, because no participant is that articulate, but real disputes over who gets to play with what, and when. Jessica's mother is trying to make order of chaos and settle the disputes. Every child seems to be crying at once. What happened to the birthday party?

Jerry's mother has just started to work. For the first time in four years he is staying for most of the day with a babysitter. It's a long day for Jerry, because he is unhappy. He cries when his mother leaves him at the babysitter's, and he seems angry when his father comes to pick him up. He refuses to look at his father and resists getting his things together to leave. Neither parent knows what to do about his seeming rejection of them.

To many people, children are mysterious. Why do they reject the friendly advances of blood relatives, throw tantrums at birthday parties, and refuse to greet their parents after hours of separation? Parents are often surprised by some new turn in development and disappointed that other changes have not yet occurred. Even highly educated parents are not sure what to expect next. Is my child precocious or retarded in talking, thinking, being toilet trained? What should I do to make sure my child is going to be normal?

This chapter describes some of the normal developments in babies and pre-school children, in the hope that knowing what to expect will help parents through difficult moments with their young children. We also hope that parents can accept the inevitable rough spots in their relationships with their youngsters without feeling that the child will be forever damaged. Children are not damaged by occasional upsets but by continually oppressive or depriving environments that no parent reading this book would be likely to inflict on a child.

Although the descriptions of normal development apply to average children across the pre-school period, we want to emphasize how different perfectly normal children are from one another. Normal children vary widely in their rates of development of motor skills, intelligence, and personality. All that we say should be adapted to *your* child's rate of development, which may be a bit faster or slower than most. Also, children are just *different* from one another, especially in temperament. Some are shy, others bold; some active, others quiet; some confident, others less so. Respect for individual differences is in our view the cornerstone of good parent-child relationships.

Infants

Newborn babies

More research on the capabilities of newborn babies has been done in the last fifteen years than in all the rest of human history. Not so long ago, experts and parents thought that newborn babies could not see or hear and that their worlds were a 'blooming buzzing confusion' (William James, 1890). Now we see them as well organized and equipped to experience the world outside the womb in their own way. The organization of newborn behaviour is quite different from that of older babies, children and adults, but a new baby is not a random processor of information.

Newborn babies see, hear, smell, taste, and feel touches and pin pricks. Their senses are not as acute as they will be in a few months, but they are capable of sensing their worlds. They are likely to see with one eye at a time in the first few weeks, because the eyeballs have not completed their rotation from the side of the head in the embryo to the front of the face, which gives humans binocular vision. Their eyes see with an acuity of about 20/200, which is quite a blur for fine details but adequate for large and close objects. Their visual acuity improves rapidly, so that by two months old they see quite well near and far.

Parents are often surprised that newborn babies seem to be tracking moving objects with their eyes. Yes, they are attracted to moving objects and can follow them as they move across their line of sight. New babies are also interested in staring at faces or any other complicated object, because nature has 'wired' them to look for information in their worlds. Newborn babies can look for long periods of time when they are awake, alert and feeling satisfied. Of course, those conditions are met only about 10 per cent of the time in their first few weeks of life.

From the first hours after birth, babies show a strong preference for sweet tastes. Lewis Lipsitt (1977) of Brown University has shown that newborn babies suck faster and harder to get a taste of sugar water than to get plain water, and that they seem disappointed when sweet water is followed by plain water. Their disappointment is gauged by the fact that they suck less vigorously for plain water *after* they have tasted sweet than if they were given plain water first. Human babies arrive in the world with a built-in sweet tooth that, as we all know, persists into adulthood.

Newborn babies dislike the same ugly smells and bitter tastes that adults find obnoxious. They turn their heads away from sulphurous odours and make grimacing faces when given a small drop of bitter liquid. In other words, their senses are tuned to the human ranges of pleasure and discomfort when they arrive in the world.

At birth and for the first couple of months, babies' behaviour is controlled by the lower and midbrain centres, not by the upper cortical brain. Think of the brain as having three layers. The lowest brain stem at the junction of the head and neck controls bodily functions such as heartbeat, digestion and automatic breathing. This part of the brain is most mature at birth, for obvious reasons.

The midbrain, which is the layer covering the brain stem, regulates emotions, reflexes such as startling and withdrawing from painful stimuli, much of vision and other senses, awakeness, and much other behaviour that is not voluntary. The midbrain is moderately mature at birth, but it will not become adult-like for some months. The neocortex, or outer layer of the brain, located just under the skull, is the centre of thinking, decision-making, motor coordination and speech – none of which newborn babies are good at. The neocortex is very immature at birth and will not fully mature until puberty, although 90 per cent of brain growth is achieved by the time the child is six. In the newborn, the cortex is hardly functioning, if at all.

For the first few months after birth, babies' behaviour is largely controlled by subcortical regions of the brain. Their actions are regulated by reflexes, a set of nearly automatic responses to the world. Babies suck in a well-organized pattern that expresses milk from the mother's nipple. They do not have to think about how to suck and get food; evolution has equipped all mammals (kittens, puppies, chimps and so forth) with a sucking reflex that manages the situation nicely. They learn more about how hard and how fast to suck in the following months. Through learning, they can adjust the strength and rate of their sucks to the flow of milk from bottle or breast. But the sucking reflex is a midbrain achievement of evolutionary history that is set off by any object inserted in the mouth.

Newborn babies have many other reflexes that serve them well. They turn their heads toward the side on which their cheeks are touched. This helps them to find the nipple in breastfeeding. They withdraw their legs and arms from painful heat and sharp objects; they turn their heads if something covers their noses and mouths; they swipe with their fists to remove any covering that threatens to block their breathing passages. They close their eyes when a fast-moving object approaches them. In other words, they have a set of reflexively organized patterns of behaviour that keeps them relatively safe from accidental harm.

New babies also have reflexes that are evolutionary hangovers without apparent usefulness in the human scheme of things. They fan their toes when the soles of their feet are stroked; they move in water with coordinated swimming movements, and they hold their breaths under water! A newborn baby must be picked up out of the water in a few seconds or he will *smother*, not drown. If you are planning to 'teach' your new baby to swim, be careful. Her reflexes will give you the impression that she is swimming easily, but remember that her aquatic equipment does not include gills to breathe under water.

New babies make walking movements when their feet are placed on a hard surface. First-time parents are amazed when the baby shows such coordination, but don't be surprised when this achievement is lost at about three months. At that age, the baby's higher cortex begins to function and takes over control from the lower centres. Humans have big cortical brains that allow us to make voluntary decisions and to learn in a far more flexible way than other mammals. Reflexive walking, swimming, toe-fanning, and many other reflexes disappear under layers of cortical control, to develop again in later years as voluntary movements.

This transformation from newborn reflexes to cortically controlled behaviour is perfectly normal for the human species. Our babies are born with immature brains, because if their heads were any bigger they would not get through the mother's pelvis. So nature has left higher brain growth to the postnatal period of infancy and childhood, which fits nicely with our careful caretaking of infants. We carry them around because they cannot yet walk; we feed and clothe them because they cannot yet do these essential things for themselves. As their brains become more mature, they learn how they are supposed to manage these tasks for themselves.

As the cortex sprouts its dendrites (nerve fibres) and grows its synaptic connections, information is transmitted from one part of the brain to another. By three months, the baby's behaviour starts on its developmental path toward adulthood. It's a long trip from the beginning of cortical behaviour to adolescent rebellion and moral judgement, but it's a fascinating one that every parent has the opportunity to observe.

Social development

Babies are social creatures. Newborn babies come equipped with a desire to be handled, soothed and carried around by caregivers.

Being picked up can quiet the noisiest newborn baby, at least most of the time. Primate babies, including our own, do not take kindly to long periods of isolation from contact with others. Human babies protest when they are put down in the cot and make clear their preference for being in close proximity to other people. New babies are alert to interesting sights and sounds, which also serve to stop their crying. Put a crying baby on your shoulder so that she can look around the room, and the chances are she will stop crying to scan the room and to snuggle on your chest.

Evolution has built into primate infants a responsiveness to close contact and the ability to protest against isolation in such noxious ways that adults will come running to turn off the crying. Infant crying raises parents' blood pressure and makes them very anxious. We are built to find infant distress very distressing. Parents sometimes think of newborn babies as helpless creatures, but in fact parents' behaviour is much more under the infant's control than the reverse. Does he come running when you cry?

Baby smiles. Even if newborn smiles are subcortical, parents are enchanted. Soon after birth babies smile – not at parents, but as they are dropping off to sleep. Smiles in the first few weeks of life occur most often when babies are drowsy and content. By about six weeks of age, there is the dawning of smiles to people: babies begin to smile at human faces and other interesting animated objects. Although parents might not like to think so, young babies are equally likely to smile at any face, not just their devoted parents', and they are just about as likely to smile at the wallpaper and the refrigerator.

The reason for this is two-fold. First, infants seem to be wired by evolution to smile at visually interesting sights, of which the human face is one. Second, babies under three or four months old do not know one face from another. They simply do not have enough working cortex to remember the faces of people they have seen before, such as mother and father. Given the uncertainty about whether people are old acquaintances or new visitors, the brain's instruction is to smile at everyone. Thus, adults observe that four- and five-month-olds are virtual smiling machines – smile and say 'hello' to the baby and you get back an utterly charming toothless grin, whether you are her mother or a total stranger.

Not all babies are equally smiley. Some light up for every face they see. Others need to be enticed to smile by animated voices, nodding heads and big adult smiles. Of course, smiling depends on how the baby is feeling at the moment. Just like any of us, being grumpy, tired, hungry or just bored makes babies less likely to light up in smiles.

Babies' smiles are very appealing to parents. When their baby smiles, parents smile back without thinking. When the baby begins to smile socially at two months, most parents feel rewarded at last for all the effort they have put into caregiving over the first two months. They feel warm all over and conclude that the pain of parenthood is worth it, even if they have just walked the floor for two hours with the baby screaming in their ears. Suddenly there is a relationship with another sensate human being who gives back some rewards – smiles of gratitude, perhaps?

Fear of strangers. It is not until about five months that most babies begin to smile more at familiar than at strange adults. (They may still smile at strange children, who are not as threatening as adults they don't know.) What is happening is that the baby's memory is improving as the brain becomes myelinized. Every nerve fibre in the brain is developing a fatty covering, called a myelin sheath, that greatly improves the transmission of impulses and the storage of experiences. Once memory develops so that the baby can remember familiar people, another routine in the evolved developmental programme says 'Beware of strangers, once you can make the distinction!' This instruction comes into play between five and eight months in human infants, somewhat earlier in monkeys and chimps.

When Granny comes to visit, many parents of eight- or nine-month-olds are embarrassed to discover that their baby is no longer willing to let Granny hold her. She used to smile at Granny, who said how adorable she was. Now she protests when her grandmother approaches and wails when she is picked up. Granny asks what *you* have done to the baby to make her so afraid. Did you let some stranger scare her?

You haven't done anything. Fear of strangers is a normal part of development in the second half of the first year. Most infants of this age resist attention from people they don't know well. Unless

Grandmother is a frequent visitor to the household, the baby will not remember her and will classify her as a stranger. Remember, we are dealing with a very immature brain. At this age, infants will observe a stranger with interest at a distance but will most often be distressed if the person gets too close.

The companion piece of fear of strangers is the attachment babies develop to their caregivers, discussed in Chapter 4. An eight-month-old is quite likely to want to follow parents around the house, protesting should he lose sight of them. Both attachment and fear of strangers result from significant changes in babies' memory and thinking abilities.

Implications for child care. The child-care implications of this long description of the human baby are that caregiving in the first two months of life can be managed perfectly well by any competent person, and the baby will be none the wiser. Young babies need rapid responses to their discomforts. Even if they do recognize some smells and sounds of familiar caregivers, they show no preference for familiar over unfamiliar caregivers in this period. Even in the next three months, babies show little if any preference for particular caregivers; they smile indiscriminately at everyone.

Thus, if you are contemplating putting your baby into day care, the first five months may be a good period in which to do it with the least upset to the baby. When she becomes mature enough to recognize individual people, she will become simultaneously familiar with parents and other caregivers. We recognize that this is radically different advice from the usual expert opinion, which calls on mothers to stay at home with their babies for at least the first year, but we think that most of that advice is based on obsolete notions of mothers and babies and on erroneous information about the nature of newborn babies and young infants.

Not until about eight to ten months do babies come to prefer strongly the company of familiar people. If at that point their mothers go back to work for the first time, babies can be pretty distressed. If babies are already familiar with other adult caregivers, there is usually less upset. Even if babies are familiar with their everyday caregivers, however, they may still express a strong preference for one or both parents and protest against being left in the morning. The six-month-old who smiled at the caregiver each morning can develop suddenly into a screaming protestor, who rejects the familiar caregiver and clings desperately to the parents when they leave for work. Peeling a crying baby off your clothing every morning is a very depressing experience, one that sends many mothers off to work in tears. Caregivers feel rejected, and parents become suspicious about their care arrangement. It is difficult to understand how a previously happy baby has turned into a seemingly insecure, desperate little waif.

You need to be philosophical about this 'separation anxiety' unless you want the baby's company twenty-four hours a day for the half-year from eight to about fifteen months. Even if mothers are home full time, most babies in the age group protest against being left in their cots for a nap, cry desperately when parents leave them with a babysitter, and demand their attachment figures in full view at all times. With an unfamiliar babysitter, the baby's protest may go on for an hour or more; with a familiar caregiver, he is likely to settle into his usual friendly relationship a few minutes after parents leave.

But parents suffer when their babies protest at separation. The combination of guilt about working and guilt about the baby's unhappiness at your leaving can be devastating, unless you understand the temporary, developmental nature of his protest. No permanent harm will come from temporary separations, no matter how loudly he cries. There is just nothing you can do but keep your friendly calm and wait until he gets a better brain that can remember that you are coming back in the afternoon. If you and the caregiver both understand what the crying means, and how short-lived it is, you can grin and bear the morning scene, knowing that he will settle into a pleasant day at the caregivers' and be glad to see you on your return.

Cognitive development

Baby experiments. New memory and thinking abilities also bring new ways of learning about the physical world. Babies around a year of age are practical scientists. They experiment with things around them, trying out various ways to use and abuse household objects and toys. Putting Dad's underwear in the toilet and pulling the roll of toilet paper all over the house are ways of finding out what happens to what objects with what actions. Parents are not enchanted with the results of unsupervised baby experiments, but the babies probably learn a great deal from them. They can learn just as much from a flannel in the bath and a ball of string to pull around and watch unravel, which makes less of a mess for the adults to deal with. But babies do need to try out their actions on the world to learn what they can do. Because safety is important, baby experiments need adult supervision.

Out of sight is out of mind. It is hard to imagine a world in which people and objects that are out of sight are literally gone. As children we may have debated whether or not the tree that falls alone in the great forest made any sound. In this debate children are confused by the idea of sound, which seems to require both sound waves and a human perceiver. The tree fell, which invariably makes sound waves, but there was no one to hear it. A baby's version of this paradox is that whatever is out of sight (or sound or smell) no longer exists.

If you have a six- to nine-month-old at home, try the following little experiment. Choose a toy or piece of food that your baby likes (biscuits work well). Have a handkerchief or dishtowel ready. Seat the baby in his highchair and interest him in the toy or food. Gently remove it from his hand and tell him you are going to hide it under the cloth and see if he can find it. Do just that. Cover the item with the cloth in his full view.

If he was really interested in the toy or biscuit and wants it back, he will cry because it has gone. If he was less interested, he will merely look at you to see what's supposed to happen next. In either case, so far as your baby is concerned the hidden item has simply gone. He will not search for it under the cloth, even if it makes a nice lump that is clearly visible to all. He will not reach for it, even if a small part of it is visible to him. Try that, too.

The importance of this experiment is to demonstrate that babies under about a year have little idea that people or things that are not in sight still exist. Is it any wonder that your baby crawls after you from room to room and protests when left with a babysitter? How can he know that you have not disappeared forever? It's not worth feeling guilty about this kind of distress, as it will pass in a few months. Furthermore, all babies experience some distress about lost people and objects. There is no way around it unless you never leave your baby's side, day and night.

Fortunately, babies' brains mature. They do get the idea that parents and favourite toys are still in the world when not visible to them. But it is not until they are about eighteen months of age that they fully realize that things they put away yesterday have not disappeared forever. Mothers learn that the baby's toys that are put away for a couple of weeks are as interesting as new toys when reintroduced. The baby's memory system has its advantages as well as disadvantages.

Can babies be spoiled?

In the first three months of life, babies *cannot* be spoiled in the sense that they learn how to manipulate parents. At this tender age, they simply have not got the brain power to remember good things that happened and to ask for them again. However many times one picks the crying baby up to console her, she will not suppose that you will pick her up again, because she simply does not know what happened two minutes ago.

Newborn babies demand attention and comforting because they need it NOW, not from ulterior motives. Meeting babies' demands is often not convenient for parents, but it's not fair to attribute mean intentions to the baby. Young babies cannot be spoiled and manipulate parents, because subcortical beings are not that clever.

From three months old, babies begin to have better memories (Cohen, 1979). By four or five months, it is possible for them to recall that when they last cried father came to play. Then it is possible for parents and the baby to set up some patterns of interaction that parents regret. In our society, where, peculiarly, infants sleep alone in their own rooms rather than with their mothers, parents do not usually cherish interactions in the small hours. And parents do not have to conform to the baby's wishes, which by four to five months of age are not real needs, for food, changing, or play in the middle of the night. They *can* learn to be daytime people.

Training babies to meet parents' schedules can be painful, because some are determined night people, just like some adults, while others slip easily into daytime activities and sleep through the night. Parental determination and patient good humour to keep the baby up during the day, filling his life with interesting interactions (otherwise known as wearing him out), will often suffice to keep him asleep at night. A few sleepless nights of hearing him cry for parental company may do the trick in most cases, for parents who can bear the experience. But some babies are extremely difficult to encourage into sleeping through the night: it's a very common problem, and one which devastates parents. Regular broken nights are too much for everyone, and one night-waking baby can undermine the whole household. If you have one of these, *don't* blame yourself. One of us carried out a study of children with sleeping problems, which showed that most of the babies who at one year were exhausting their parents by their regular waking (roughly a third of the sample of eighty babies) had been the lively jumpy babies *from birth* (Dunn, 1980). Their sleeplessness at fourteen months old was not a simple consequence of their parents' child-rearing techniques. Rather, it was one aspect of a particularly lively (and sometimes irritable) personality. It takes a very tough parent to win a let-him-cry-it-out battle with one of these babies.

And babies need adult attention to develop into real human beings. The sad plight of orphanage infants, left to cry in their cots day and night, is no joke. Babies want and need people to smile at them, talk to them and play with them. Parents can decide whether they'll be with their babies principally in the daylight or moonlight hours, but of course they should not expect to ignore their baby's need for holding and loving interactions both day and night. Human babies are primates who have evolved to be stimulated and held much of the time in order to develop normally.

Play with other babies?

Parents often wonder if it will be good for their baby to spend time with other babies. Playing with other children sounds like a good idea. Does it *help* the baby's development? Some babies and toddlers are certainly interested in other babies, though others appear to ignore them and just head for the toys that the other child has. To really *play* with another toddler, very young children have to be extremely familiar with one another. If two children have been 'baby-minded' with one another since the early months, they do indeed begin to play together by the end of the first year, and by eighteen months can show a touching concern for the other child's distress (as well as a blithe disregard for the other's wishes). But cooperation over play is unusual before about eighteen months. In the first two years of life, babies notice one another. They pat and make noises at each other. They may even share a toy, and in the second year will watch closely what the other does with it (Eckerman and Whatley, 1977; Eckerman, Whatley and Kutz, 1975). There are few sustained exchanges where the children take turns. There are only occasional meetings of the minds in the first eighteen months.

So being with other babies is not really important to a baby's development, in the way that being with adults is. It is not *harmful*, and if your baby sees a few children very regularly, he may well get a lot of pleasure and interest from them. Think of the young siblings that you know. Some babies get really excited and happy when their pre-school aged siblings appear: they are a delightful audience for their brothers and sisters, and by the second year are compliant companions in play (Dunn, 1983; Dunn, 1984). Other brothers and sisters are of course not such happy friends, and it is a no-holds-barred battle from morning to night. It's pretty clear to parents that for these siblings it is being *away* from each other that is likely to be beneficial . . .

The play of infants and toddlers is like fleeting conversations at a cocktail party. First, I say something. You may listen but fail to respond because someone else has got your attention. Meanwhile, I have been distracted by an old friend who just came in. Our interaction is brief, and it is terminated before it has got anywhere. Older children's interactions are more like a long dinner party with a few friends. There is time and interest to sustain the conversation and the games.

In many cultures, older children are given the primary care of the under-threes; they carry them around and take them off their backs when they play with other child caretakers. Adults probably do a better job with young children than babies' older siblings do, because children of six to twelve have their own agendas. But we have no research to compare the advantages that adults and older children have to offer. That we have no research on this issue is not accidental. The question was not asked, because the concept was unthinkable. Mothers were supposed to stay home.

Babies in the first year and a half of life change remarkably from mindless sensers to deliberate actors. As their brains mature, they come to experience the world of things and people in more continuous fashion – they remember what has happened before and know familiar people. Relationships between parents and babies develop and, with parental patience, are great sources of joy for both.

Toddlers

Toddlers between the ages of eighteen and thirty-six months are both adorable and annoying to many parents. Here the battles begin. The baby/child emphatically says 'No,' and the parent is offended. How can this twenty-six-inch-tall monster tell me what he will and will not do? Parents take the toddler literally and retaliate. Toddlers are taken too seriously because they speak the language, or at least some of it.

Learning to speak the language is a major advance in child development. The child can now communicate more effectively than when she muttered 'muk' to show that she was thirsty. Toddlers so often utter devastating phrases, such as 'Me no go!' and 'No want sausage!' in response to their parents' earnest pleas to leave the playground and eat lunch. How unreasonable of the baby/child to have opinions! And really, how unreasonable of parents to take them so seriously that bad feelings are created.

Adults are crucial for toddlers

Toddlers are emotionally still almost dependent on adult emotional support. Some may have important relationships with other children – siblings especially – but it is adult love, approval, interaction and interpretation of the world that they need. Two-year-olds at a birthday party of other two-year-olds who they don't know well are typically more interested in the toys than in the other children, who serve more as competitors than as companions. Thus a party that seems to be going well can suddenly dissolve into pools of toddler tears when competition over favoured toys erupts. Three- and four-year-olds have not only better social skills but much greater interest in playmates than toddlers, who are still concerned most with adult attention.

When primate babies get past the infant state, they insist on climbing down off the mother's back or lap and venturing a short way from her to explore the world. As they get older and braver, they venture further. Danger lurks out there, so they scurry back and forth to the safety of the adult. Emotionally, primate babies need their caregivers as islands of safety from which to explore. As they get older, they feel secure with separations over greater times and distances, and they play more often and more intensely with other young ones.

Human toddlers can be shy or brave and can vacillate from state to state. Some two-year-olds do not even look at the people in a strange place for at least ten minutes after arrival. It may take twenty minutes before they tiptoe out from behind an adult to explore the toys and other attractions. Other children run headlong into new experiences, whatever they are, disregarding dangers to their very lives. Children who are brave in the grocer's shop may shrink with fear at having to undress in the clinic. Whoever they are, toddlers need adults behind them for courage.

It is adults who give meaning to children's experiences and help them to learn about the world (Bruner, 1983). A fire engine is just a noisy scary unlabelled thing unless some adult tells the two-year-old it's a fire engine that rushes to the fire with hoses and brave firefighters who battle with the blaze and save the occupants. Travelling on a train to London past stations, bridges, rivers and canals is uninterpretable to a two-year-old unless an adult gives her words and a context for the sights. Some of the best-travelled young children in the world are the children of migrant farmworkers. Unfortunately, too often they are not told where they are or where they've been. To begin to make sense of the jumble of impressions, they need adults who describe and explain and answer questions.

On the positive side, two-year-olds are some of the most charming people in the world. They have honest relationships with people; some they like and some they don't. What more should we ask? They are intensely involved in play; cars go 'Vroom, Vroom!' on the floor, aeroplanes soar over the coffee table, and dollies get their cold-infested noses wiped. Toddlers are disarming in their openness and not to be taken too literally. If one thinks of them as older babies, one can overlook their challenges to authority, enjoy their disarming honesty, and see them as emerging children.

Toddlers are aware that there are right and wrong ways to do things, by adult standards (Kagan, 1981). Broken toys and spilled milk evoke 'uh-oh' sounds of discomfort. One item on the Bayley Test of Mental Development for toddlers capitalizes on their concern about violations of adult standards. A small doll with the head severed from the body is shown to the child. 'Oh, look!' says the examiner. 'The dolly is broken. Can you fix her?' Two-year-olds respond with interest and concern. They all try to put the head back on the doll, sometimes backwards or upside down, but they all try.

Two-year-olds also have an emerging sense of self. They recognize their reflections in a mirror, not as another child but as 'me'. 'Me' is, of course, a favourite word, used almost as often as 'no'. The significance of 'me' cannot be exaggerated, because it signals the child's growing sense of himself as a person with likes and dislikes, needs and wishes. The toddler's explorations in selfhood are at the root of many conflicts with parents, whose wishes do not always coincide with the child's.

Confrontations and life with two-year-olds

The so-called Terrible Twos got their reputation from the overuse of the word 'no'. 'Do you want to go to the shops with Mummy?' 'No.' 'Shall we take a nap now?' 'No.' Parents who ask such questions are really asking for it; toddlers are big on rejecting adult demands, especially when they are couched in questions that seem to request the child's cooperation. It seems that some toddlers keep their parents frustrated and completely under their thumbs: the trick is to ignore the literal challenge to one's authority and sanity.

Toddlers don't mean 'no' literally. They mean it figuratively – at least we should take it that way.

The adult challenge is to distract and co-opt the little one. Don't confront. You will lose to their temper tantrums and consume vast amounts of emotional energy that you need for daily living. It is no contest for adults to overpower a thirty-pound being with an immature brain. Some parents are tempted to beat toddlers into submission, but this is surely a losing proposition, both in the short and long runs. There is no reason to confront them at all. Just outmanoeuvre them.

The most dangerous part of the confrontation of toddlers with their parents is that the baby/child sometimes gets battered. In extreme cases, they get scalded in boiling water, burned with cigarettes, and beaten so severely that they sustain brain damage and broken bones. Outraged parents think they are teaching the baby a lesson. In less extreme cases, toddlers get spanked and yelled at, when the child cannot possibly understand why. Toddlers do not learn constructive lessons from abuse by their parents. They learn to cower anxiously in their parents' presence and later to take it out on playmates.

Your toddler does not want to leave the playground. 'Do you know what we are going to do? Go to the shop, and you can have a big banana. Will you help me find the bananas at the shop? Do you remember where they were last time?' By this time the baby/child is so engrossed in conversation that he has not noticed that you have walked most of the way towards your destination. Toddlers need gentle physical management.

No marmite for lunch? How about peanut butter? Eggs and toast? Why not let the toddler decide what she wants for tea? That's one sphere in which she can safely make decisions among a large number of equally nutritious possibilities. Why make a battle of it?

Don't ask questions you don't want answers to. Don't ask if the child wants to go to Grandmother's with you, unless you are ready to accept 'NO!' for an answer. Tell him you are going and that there will be something good for him in it. If there isn't something attractive to him about the visit, provide something. Visiting Grandmother is not a moral Rubicon for a two-year-old.

Don't ask if the child wants to have a bath, when you know she hates being washed. Just pick her up and announce that it is time for a bath and that you have something special for her to play with in the water. A new submarine or rubber duck can do wonders for the baby/child's aversion to baths. If she continues to protest, you will just have to bathe her. There is no point in getting angry about it. Maybe she doesn't need a bath every day. How about a couple of times a week and a lot of spot-cleaning?

The principles for dealing with toddlers are (1) not to take them too seriously, and (2) to co-opt whenever possible. Do not assume that the words that come out of the mouth are intentionally defiant. If you do assume so, you're likely to be offended often. Why put yourself through that when your child, like all others, will grow into a more reasonable three- and four-year-old? A little distance and forbearance would avoid most of the clashes that mar the relationships of parents and their two-year-olds.

Three-year-olds

Three-year-olds turn the corner from babyhood into childhood. They usually speak the language well enough to make their opinions known, ask endless questions, and sometimes listen to the answers. They like to be read stories, to watch TV, and to play with other children. They are much less shy with adults than they have been since about nine months of age. They do not know all the adult rules of conduct, but the mistakes they make are less naive than those they made the previous year. Instead of pouring the flowers and water on the floor so he can use the vase as a spaceship, a three-year-old is more likely to paint the base purple as a birthday present for his mother. At least he recognizes that he should give her something.

It is easy to overestimate what a three-year-old knows and can do. It is easy, especially with first children, to expect them to make giant strides in dressing, tying shoes, telling the time, and remembering instructions. Just because they talk pretty well doesn't mean they can keep three instructions in mind in the right order. Three-year-olds are more logical than twos. They use the 'why . . . because' construction constantly. They are often incorrect, by adult standards, in the conclusions they reach, but adults have the feeling that they are dealing with a thinking animal. Two-year-olds seem more like feeling animals.

It is also easy to underestimate what a three-year-old knows and can do. One of the foremost researchers on pre-school children's intelligence, Rochel Gelman of the University of Pennsylvania, reports her surprise at what young children know about numbers and quantities. She and her collaborators have shown that three-year-olds honour the principles of counting and estimating quantities, even if they do not yet use adult terms (Gelman and Gallistel, 1978; Gelman, 1979).

According to Gelman, counting objects successfully requires the application of five principles in coordination: (1) the one-to-one principle – each item in an array must be tagged with one and only one unique word; (2) the stable order principle – the words assigned must be drawn from a stably ordered list (*one, two, three . . ., un, deux, trois . . .*); (3) the cardinal principle – the last word in the array signals the total number in the array; (4) the abstraction principle – any collection of items may be counted, whether they are balls, dogs, poker chips, or a mixture of all three; and (5) the order-irrelevance principle – the order in which items in an array are tagged is irrelevant as long as the other principles are honoured.

Counting is intellectually far more complicated than most of us imagined! However, most three-year-olds adhere to the five principles and count small arrays successfully. They may use their own lists of number terms, such as *one, six, ten*, or *two, ball, bear*, but they use the same words in the same order and apply them to each item in the array, regardless of order. The last word signals the total count, just as it should, even if most adults do not understand the word.

Young children make errors in language of much the same kind they make in counting: they know the principles but they don't always apply them correctly. In fact, their errors in speech tell us that they *do* know the rules. In English, the past tense, for example, is usually formed by adding *ed* to the end of the present tense verb, so that 'look' becomes 'looked', 'cook' becomes 'cooked'. Many common verbs in English are irregular, however. The past tense of 'go' is 'went', of 'do' is 'did'.

Two-year olds often have the correct past tense form as part of their vocabularies. They can say, 'Mummy went to work' and 'Daddy did the dishes'. Older pre-schoolers who used to say certain past tenses correctly may begin to make mistakes by making regular past tenses of irregular verbs ('Mummy goed to work' and 'Daddy doed the dishes'). Such mistakes are often annoying to parents, who cannot imagine where the child learned such improper speech.

Mistakes of this kind indicate that the child has learned important *rules* of the native tongue. Knowing the rule for past tenses is an advance over learning each one separately as part of one's vocabulary. The child's mistake is to overgeneralize the past tense rule. Fortunately, once they have mastered the rule, children go on to learn the irregular verb forms, but often not until they are in the six- to eight-year-old range.

Plural forms show a similar pattern. Add an *s* to the singular, and an English plural is formed – most of the time. 'Foots', 'mouses', and 'deers' abound in young children's speech. Adult correction is not very influential. First, it seems, children have to master the rule, and then they will consider exceptions.

Three-year olds, as recent research shows us, have quite striking intellectual capabilities. Such young children are able to apply their skills to only very limited problems, however. Their limitations come from three sources: problems with complexity, their inability to give long attention to solving problems, and their poor assessment of their own knowledge. Three- and four-year-olds can count small arrays, such as two and three items; they cannot count twenty- and twenty-five-item arrays. There are just too many items for them to count accurately. Although they understand the principles of counting, they cannot keep the routine going long enough to get it right.

Part of the problem that pre-school children have with counting large arrays is the second limitation on their performance: attention. Young children are easily distracted. More important is the fact that they cannot 'will' themselves to pay attention as well as school-age children can. Parents notice that three-year-olds can watch 'Sesame Street' straight through the hour without wavering attention, but if asked to straighten out a messy toy box, their attention wanders after thirty seconds. This observation does not mean that young children are wilfully uncooperative. Rather, it means that they are victims of external attractions.

Some television programmes are made very attractive to young children by presenting short, rapidly moving sequences and ever-changing episodes. Research on children's television watching shows this to be a successful attention-getting strategy. Whether such fast-paced, hypnotizing television fare is good for young children has been questioned (Singer and Singer, 1982). Does the child build up the expectation that his attention will be captured by all learning materials, rather than learning to pay attention? Books do not change colours or images in milliseconds, or repeat words in rapid succession. Some experts now argue that slower-paced television fare that allows children time to think about the material is more valuable than the faster-paced programmes that merely capture their attention.

There is no argument, however, that young children have trouble paying attention. Being asked to empty and reorganize a toy box is neither attention-getting nor attractive to many children. They prefer to play with a few toys and to leave the others on the floor. Their inability to control attention is a real liability. Even though they want to please their parents, they simply cannot always attend to a task long enough to do what has been asked. In many cases, parents overestimate what a young child can do.

The third limitation of young children's abilities is a lack of self-monitoring. They do not know what they know and what they don't know (Flavell *et al.*, 1981). John Flavell asked pre-school children to follow instructions in building block towers. Some of the instructions were garbled, because the person giving the instructions coughed or sneezed in the middle. Others were impossible to carry out because there were no rectangular blue blocks in the child's pile.

Older children responded by asking for a repeat of the instructions when coughs or sneezes interrupted them. They told the investigator that the task was impossible when the required blocks were not in the pile. Three- and four-year-olds proceeded with the tasks as best as they could until they got stuck and didn't know what to do next. They did not anticipate trouble with the instructions until they got to the point of difficulty. The contrast of school-age children with three- and four-year-olds is that the older children ask themselves questions about what they do and do not know *before* they proceed. Three- and four-year-olds are likely to go ahead until they get stuck. This shows a lack of foresight about what they know, and it gets in the way.

Anyone who has ever planned a project with a pre-school child can resonate to this research. 'Let's build an aeroplane!' As soon as the first piece of balsa wood and paintbrush are put on the work bench, the child is ready to paint. Never mind that the plane has to be built first, before the paint goes on. The pre-school child is all action – ready or not, here I come!

Four-year-olds

Four-year-olds are real children, not babies. When people think of pre-school children, they are probably thinking of four-year-olds and imagining such things as a group sitting in a circle on a rug listening with rapt attention to the teacher reading *Curious George* or *Where the Wild Things Are*; finger paintings, still wet, brought home proudly from school; trips to the natural history museum for enthusiastic dinosaur lovers; and real conversations about feelings – all typical four-year-old activities.

Four-year-olds are more independent and competent in the worldly ways of older children than three-year-olds. Their mastery of the language is very good, with the exception of certain irregularities previously noted. They are secure in their knowledge of themselves as boys and girls. And they are eager to play with other children and to begin more formal educational activities. Parents and nursery-school teachers love four-year-olds, because they are amenable to many adult-directed activities and their control of attention is much better than that of three-year-olds. But it is easy to overestimate their emotional maturity and be surprised when they cry on the first day at play group or nursery school.

The logic of four-year-olds is more officially adult than that of younger pre-school children. 'If . . . then' statements begin to be uttered. 'If I clean up my room, then will you take me to (fill in the latest craze)?' They begin to cut through some of the hazy distinctions between fantasy and reality that confuse younger children. Dreams are now less real and scary than they were; what the child fears or wants might not actually come true, in his own view. Thinking does not make things happen.

By four to five, children become much better at understanding how things work. Their cause-effect knowledge adheres to adult standards more closely, though not perfectly, and they are curious about what makes engines run, why aeroplanes fly, and why frogs can't just walk like us. They are more orientated to the outer world of neighbourhood, friends and school, as the illuminating studies of London and Nottingham four-year-olds carried out by Barbara Tizard and Martin Hughes and the Newsons show so vividly (Newson and Newson, 1968; Tizard and Hughes, 1984).

It is not an accident that in most cultures of the world, children begin their apprenticeships for adulthood around the age of five. Four is really the end of early childhood, and five the beginning of readiness for training of at least a limited sort. We and other western European nations begin formal school the year the child turns five. Most experts agree that by four, children are ready for group experience and a limited amount of formal instruction.

Relationships of four-year-olds with other children are tentative. Friendships are often fleeting. Parents should not be surprised that their four-year-old has a succession of friends of both sexes. At this age, children's friendships are based on shared time and interests, not on more profound psychological understanding of each others' needs and concerns (Berndt, 1981).

Sex differences are well established in the minds and behaviour of pre-school girls and boys. They know who is who and what is supposed to be what. Boys are not supposed to play with dolls, at least not much, and girls are. Boys are supposed to be strong and brave, and girls are not, even though boys are not physically stronger at this age than girls. Girls feel freer than boys to cross the stereotyped sex lines and to play with and like boys. Nonetheless, four-year-olds foreshadow the division of the sexes that is so prominent in elementary school. In pre-school, too, boys play more with boys and girls with girls (Garvey, 1979), although friendships cross gender lines to a much greater extent than in later childhood.

Pre-school children need adults, too

Emotionally, three- and four-year-olds are still very adult-orientated (Hartup, 1983). They need adult guidance, intimate, enduring relationships with adults, and adult comfort in times of trouble. It should not be surprising that a change from having mother at home full time to spending the day with other children in a day-care situation can be upsetting to a pre-school child. Because young children are not able to reflect on their feelings very well, they often act out their anger and grief at such changes in their lives, and the anger may well be directed at you – the parent.

Fortunately, such feelings do not usually last very long – children become adjusted to the new situation and its opportunities for enjoyable activities – but we should surely take their feelings seriously, and understand them. Even if your child is not seemingly glad to see you at the end of the day, you can still express pleasure at seeing her. You can be understanding of what a big change this is in her world and of how she might feel about it. Such understanding and confidence that all will be well encourages the child to make the adjustment to a new situation. Your pleasant consideration tells her that you care about her feelings, understand her distress, and that you are sure that the day-care experience can be a good one for her. There is certainly no use in acting as though your own feelings are hurt by her temporary rejection of you. Even if your feelings are hurt, it will not pay in the long run to act on those feelings by rejecting the child or being angry. Such responses only worsen the chances of a child's adjusting well to the new environment.

Dealing with pre-school children

As babies turn into children, by metamorphosis it seems, parents find themselves dealing with more rational, more talkative, and more independent beings. Pre-school children make many of the same mistakes that two-year-olds do by confronting their parents in ways that some parents find provocative. The pre-school period is one in which children are establishing control over their own behaviour (Erikson, 1950). It's a process that starts in the two-year-old period and accelerates through the threes and fours.

Some parents find pre-school children enormously irritating, because they often challenge authority and ask stupid questions – over and over again. Three- and four-year-olds are so persistently curious that they often threaten to drive parents crazy. Will he *never* shut up?! Parental anger at being incessantly bothered can sometimes provoke outbursts of abuse. Pre-school children are prime targets for child abuse, because they do not have the judgement to know when to stop, when to back off, when to mollify an angry adult. Of course, they are not equipped with the brainpower to manage such complex social situations, so they get beaten or yelled at instead.

The same advice on managing two-year-olds goes for threes and fours, too, with the modification that parents can talk to them more and handle them less. Reasoning with a two-year-old is mostly a thankless task. Reasoning with an older pre-school child is not. Explaining *why* a family rule is the way it is or *why* the child must go to the doctor for an injection is not hopeless with four-year-olds. They may not comply immediately, but the explanation has an impact in the long run. At the very least, the parent is establishing a mode of reasonable interaction with the child that will help the relationship through the rest of childhood and adolescence.

If pre-school children do not comply with verbal instructions and explanations of essential behaviours ('Please get into the car, because we are going to the doctor's office'; 'You must get dressed now so that we can leave for the beach'), then calm physical management is still the best policy. The parent should pick the child up and do what has to be done. It is important for you not to lose your temper and get nasty about it, because this can have bad repercussions on your relationship with the child.

It is also important that young children do not win battles with parents over their noncompliance. If parents make important and reasonable demands for compliance, they should hold to those demands. Pre-school children are not the best judges of their own welfare, which is why they have parents. Parents who are cowed by temper tantrums and screaming defiance are only inviting more of the same. Few of us enjoy the experience of dragging a screaming child into the doctor's office or out of the supermarket, but sometimes it has to be done. Young children become more cooperative with parents who confidently assert the reasons for their demands and enforce reasonable rules. Even if there are a few rough spots, relationships between parents and young children run more smoothly when the parent, rather than the child, is in control.

In this chapter, we have tried to describe briefly something of the nature of babies, toddlers and pre-school children – what they can and cannot understand, do, and express. Our goal is to communicate what are reasonable expectations of young children as you consider child-care situations for them. We have also discussed some effective ways of managing young children, so that parents can avoid angry confrontations with them. The crucial point is that parents sometimes attribute too much intentionality and responsibility to young children for their actions and their words. We hope that understanding the nature of two- to four-year olds can help parents not to take all of their child's behaviour literally and to develop their own ways of dealing with it effectively.

CHAPTER SEVEN

Good Child Care by Mothers and Others

If you knew nothing about vegetable gardening, would you buy a bunch of seeds and throw them on the ground, hoping for a bumper crop this summer? Or would you talk to others with experience in gardening, in the hope that you could acquire instant expertise? Would you read gardening books with their step-by-step methods of soil preparation, planting, tending and harvesting? One advantage of the book method is that you can refer again and again to the sequence and timing of steps toward success. An advantage of going to an experienced adviser is that not all knowledge of how to succeed at gardening seems to be written down by literate experts. In one part of the country, local gardeners augment the good advice of gardening books with information about locally successful practice in clay soil and with unpredictable winters; in other parts, it is information from experienced gardeners about prevailing winds and heavy rainfall that's useful. Of course, some experienced gardeners are not really very good at growing things. In any case, it is unlikely that you would succeed at vegetable gardening without one or both kinds of knowledge.

New parents face a similar dilemma. They want their new baby to develop successfully and happily into a fully-fledged adult, but they often know little about which problems may be serious, or how best to encourage her developing skills. To support children, and to help them over difficult stages, it does help to know the outline of predictable changes from infancy to adolescence, as well as to know what your child is like as a person, and to know what he needs from you. To know a child is to understand his developmental levels of thinking, language, physical skills, and his emotional make-up – what excites, pleases or upsets him. The best world for a child to grow up in is one in which his or her experiences are happy, loving, appropriate for his age and stage, and in which the people are sensitive to his individual needs.

Many parents get some instruction on how to manage the birth of their child. Such courses inform expectant parents about the entire process by which labour and delivery proceed (with the exception of caesarean section, which will befall an unsuspecting 20 per cent of new parents). The antenatal classes do a fine job of telling pregnant parents how to manage themselves under the stress of a normal birth. Typical antenatal classes also teach about the physical care of newborn babies – how to succeed at breast-feeding, how to cut their minuscule nails, how to prevent nappy rash, and how to avoid drowning the baby in the first bath.

All of the parents' antenatal attention is focused on getting themselves through the birth and the first few days at home. The healthy baby has been delivered in a more or less satisfying fashion. It is feeding well, has short nails and a clean bottom, and has not drowned. What now? There is so much that new parents do not know about normal infant development that every day brings puzzling decisions. Is it normal for the baby to sleep six hours in a row, be awake for four hours, cry for two solid hours, be startled by a honking car horn, stare intently at your ear, smile only when asleep, throw up part of each feeding, and so on? Sympathetic doctors and Health Visitors get many, many questions from anxious parents of first babies, because new parents do not know enough about normal child development. New parents also may not know when the baby has real developmental problems, for the same reason. Without having a pattern of normal development in your heads and some sense of how babies differ from one another, how can you know when to relax and when to worry?

What Makes for Better Child Care?

The last chapter reviewed research on the nature of babies and young children. This chapter addresses how to care for infants and pre-school children. What are the qualities of good care for children as they develop, and for individual children whose needs vary? How can parents ensure that their children receive good care, both the care they provide themselves and the care they arrange for others to give? Should parents be teachers of their babies and young children? Do parents, caregivers, and teachers have different or similar roles to play in children's lives?

Experience and training of caregivers

It is often said that experience is the best teacher. What you gain from experience can depend, however, on what it teaches. Experience with babies and young children may help you (1) to know the nature of the child, (2) to understand the range of normal individual differences among children of each age, (3) to know your own child's unique constellation of physical, mental and personal characteristics, and (4) to feel more confident in dealing with your infant and young child. The experience of some parents with their children, however, seems to teach them to be intolerant and to have inappropriate expectations of children.

Most parents today, especially first-time parents, do not have years of experience with little ones. Perhaps your close friend has a baby, but your contact with the child has been limited to fleeting games before she is whisked away to bed. Going home with a new baby after two days in the hospital and no nurses to tell you how to handle things is a very different experience, and it can be a dizzying one. How are you supposed to know what to do, never mind know how to assess the states and development of this new person? The first few months of a baby's life can shake parents' self-confidence, especially if the baby's adjustment to life outside the womb is not easy.

What do you know about six-month-olds, two-year-olds, and school-age children? We are not going to say that if you trust your 'instincts' about parenting everything will turn out all right. On the contrary, it can really help parents to provide reasonable care for their children as they grow up if they know something about child development.

Although most parents today do not have much experience with babies and young children, they can read books and take courses on child development and child care. Research on day care shows that caregivers with more training in child development provide more stimulating and developmentally appropriate care for babies and young children. Most day caregivers are also parents; ergo, training helps parents, too.

Two US studies of day care in nurseries and with childminders have recently reported on the qualities of child care that are related to good child development. Researchers spent many hours observing in the nurseries and homes to evaluate the kinds of caregiver behaviour that go with better and worse outcomes for the children in their care. The National Day Care Study (Ruopp and Travers, 1982) focused on day-care centres (day nurseries). The team studied sixty-seven centres in three cities – Atlanta, Detroit and Seattle – to make sure that diverse day-care arrangements were included. The centres varied widely in staff-to-child ratios, in expenditures per child, in the training of the staff and their experience with children, and in the ethnic composition of the families whose children attended the centres. The investigators measured the children's mental and language development and observed their social behaviour in the centres.

One of the major findings concerned the qualities of caregivers. Caregivers with training in child development or early childhood education interacted more, and more constructively, with the children than other caregivers without such training. Well-trained caregivers were more likely to praise, comfort, respond, question and instruct pre-school children than caregivers with less training. The actual number of years of formal education, apart from child-related education, was not important to the kind of care given. Only the amount of education in child development contributed to being better caregivers. Children with well-trained caregivers scored better on the language and intelligence tests, and they were socially better adjusted. The number of years of experience with babies and young children did not improve child care; only child-development knowledge did.

A companion study of childminders was recently conducted and has not yet been fully reported (Ruopp and Travers, 1982). The initial results confirm those of the study of centres, however. Caregiver training is found to be important to the way the children in the day-care homes are faring. Caregivers with more training in child development engaged in more direct interaction and more educational activities with the children, and the children had higher developmental levels on tests and observations.

Nearly all these home caregivers are mothers taking care of a few children in their own homes. Many have pre-school children of their own among their charges. Knowledge of child development and child care has a positive effect on the care they give their own children, too. Other educational achievements did not seem to help. Being a college graduate in art history or chemical engineering is evidently not going to help you provide suitable care for your child, but knowing something about children will.

Size of group

Just as children fare better with well-trained caregivers, children in small groups fare better than those in larger groups.

> Results were relatively clearcut and consistent across components of the study and across sites. In groups where the absolute number of children was small, children were more cooperative and responsive to initiatives by adults and other children, more likely to engage in spontaneous verbalization and creative/intellectual activity, and less likely to wander aimlessly or to be uninvolved in activities than were children in larger groups (Ruopp and Travers, 1982, p. 81).

Small groups had advantages over larger groups even when the ratio of caregivers to children was the same. If there were fifteen three-year-olds, the children were better off with one caregiver taking charge of five children in a separate 'family' group than with all fifteen children together with three caregivers. (Usually, nature provides that human mothers have no more than three or four children below the age of five.) In the larger groups with more than one adult, the caregivers attend to each other and to other business, rather than to the children.

For infants and toddlers, group size was just as important as for the over-threes, but a small ratio of children to staff also predicted better development of the younger children. Under-threes need more one-to-one interaction with adults than do older children. The range of staff-to-child ratios in day-care centres included some that were adequate for all ages, such as 1:4, and some that were not, such as 1:10. Even a larger ratio of children to staff, such as 7:1, could be all right for over-threes, but not for babies and toddlers.

We don't yet have information on day nurseries and child-minders in Britain that compares with this American research on the effects of child-care training. We *do* have studies on nurseries and childminders that give us useful information on how parents can evaluate other features of the quality of the care in different settings, and this is discussed in Chapter 9. These British studies did examine how the size of group affected the quality of care that a child received, and found very much the same results as those reported from the American studies.

Qualities of good care

In addition to caregiver training in child development and small group size, there are other factors that make a difference in child care. Sally Provence, a professor of paediatrics at Yale, claims that good child care depends on both developmental knowledge and on how closely the care is tuned to the individual child. Although her specific reference is to nonmaternal care, we believe that what she says holds just as true within the family.

Sally Provence recommends that, in evaluating child care for babies, we be aware of two aspects: experiences that are generally appropriate to promote the development of children of that particular age, and consideration for the different needs of individual children. The point here is that some infants are adaptable to almost any situation, whereas others need more specific care conditions in order to be comfortable and to thrive. Sally Provence says:

> One might question why it is important for infant day care that constructs such as congenital characteristics, biological vulnerability, maturation and endowment be considered, since they are not at first glance a concern of the day-care planner or provider. However, acknowledging the relevance of these ideas is useful because they explain, in part, the necessity to individualize care and thus make caregivers more tolerant of the varying needs of normal infants. For example, a baby who is very sensitive to stimulation and reacts with disorganization and crying often needs quite different handling than one who is more adaptable and less sensitive (Provence, 1982, p. 38).

The sensitive baby is not abnormal or neurotic, just different from the carefree one who loves being thrown up in the air and caught at the last moment before hitting the ground. The three-year-old who prefers some time alone with puzzles or books should not be compelled to spend all of her time marching with the group banging cymbals and triangles to loud music. The world of caregiving should accommodate the different needs of different children.

As we examine the qualities of child care that encourage good development, we will encounter several lists of desirable characteristics. The lists do not conflict; they address different aspects of good care, depending on their focus – on physical, developmental or economic issues. Most lists have been drawn up to describe desirable day care, but they apply equally well to home environments. The issue is good child care, wherever it occurs.

From her experiences in managing a day-care centre for babies and young children, Sally Provence lists her requisites for good care of infants and young children, which we have here elaborated for clarity:

1. Physical care: feeding, changing, wrapping and unwrapping as the temperature demands, toileting, safety, and so forth.
2. A supportive physical environment: one in which child-size furniture and other objects accommodate the child's interests and needs, where older pre-school children can hang their coats, keep their things, and have some privacy.
3. Responsiveness to individual needs: provision of a rich variety of activities of social and nonsocial types.
4. Opportunities for the child to act on his environment: materials and opportunities to hammer, paste, colour, cut, sweep, dress, wash, build, mash, throw, kick, mix, stir, beat, pedal, run, dance, strum, jump, skip, button, zip and spit. Young children need these to feel effective and competent.
5. An enriching emotional atmosphere: good relationships with caregivers who are consistently available, affectionate, patient, good listeners, good talkers, and enthusiastic about the child's achievements. Every child deserves somebody to be excited about the first time he walks and the first time he rides a tricycle.

6. A speaking social partner: an awkward way of saying that babies and children need responsive adults who make conversation with them. Even one-year-olds learn how to take turns in a communication between two people. They may not have words, but they listen and then respond; they initiate and then wait for the partner to respond. Two- and three-year-olds need and enjoy lots of experience with transmitting messages and listening to others.
7. Experiences with consistency and repetition, variety and contrast. Everybody's world needs comforting consistency and interesting variety. Too much of the former is boring; too much of the latter is fearsome. Babies and young children, too, get bored and frightened by too much of one or the other.
8. Toys and other playthings appropriate to the developmental levels and interests of the children.
9. Quiet moments: amen.
10. Limits, prohibitions, and expectations for conformity: just as children need opportunities to express themselves, they also need to learn limits on their behaviour that will make them acceptable members of their society. Children do not come into the world knowing the social rules; adults must teach them. Firmly enforced guidlelines for behaviour, especially those aspects that affect safety and others' rights, are essential in any child-care situation.

Note that Sally Provence's list includes opportunities both for social interaction and affection and for quiet experiences with toys. It includes some constraints and limits, and opportunities for constructive action. The child in such care is free within limits to act on and explore the environment and yet is not compelled to be in constant social contact with others. In our opinion that is a reasonable set of general guidelines for child care.

Matching the Care with the Child

Babies and young children come in all varieties of shapes, sizes, abilities, personalities and interests. Why should any child be forced to fit into someone else's mould, as long as the child can thrive under some normal circumstances? Does it really matter if some children are more sociable and others more intense? Some talk less, and others are absent-minded. They are just born that way, and while parents can shape their behaviour to a considerable extent, it is much more difficult to change the whole personality and outlook of even a one-year-old. The care situation, whether at home or in a day-care setting, should accommodate the individual differences of the children, not the reverse.

A sensitive parent usually knows what these individual differences are, because the household has had to respond to the needs of its youngest member. If the baby is irritable and wakes often at night, parents have had to adjust to some sleepless nights. If the baby resents any change in schedule or hates new foods, parents have had to cope with the baby's idiosyncrasies.

Babies who are 'easy' demand far less of parents than those who are 'difficult' (Thomas and Chess, 1977). Difficult babies are irritable, reject new foods, situations and people, and fuss strenuously about their frequent complaints. Such babies are often not fun to live with, either as infants or as older children. They tend to be finicky, fussy, and trying to their parents. Easy babies are smiley, cheerful, adaptable, friendly and rewarding to parents. All babies have their fussy moments and periods of illness and teething, when their good nature is sorely tried. Moments and occasional periods of gloom do not classify a baby as difficult. Rather, babies who are classified as difficult are consistently irritable and overreactive.

If you have a difficult baby, it is far better for the child that you learn to live with his temperament. Fighting his temperament by demanding that he adjust to your expectations will only set up conflicts that can lead to later problems in his adjustment. Alexander Thomas and Stella Chess (1977) found that difficult babies grew up well in families where the parents were tolerant of their idiosyncrasies, but they did not fare well with parents who fought their needs. Difficult babies with intolerant parents were referred frequently for psychological services in pre-school and early school years, whereas those with tolerant parents were not. Easy babies did not seem to present any special problems, regardless of whether they had tolerant or intolerant parents.

In practical terms, good care for a difficult baby or young child requires a lot of patience and good parental sense about what is and what is not important. Finicky eaters can still be well nourished. Marmite and cheese for breakfast 365 days a year may not suit your ideas about gourmet dining, but it's not bad nutrition. Children do not have to eat liver, asparagus and artichokes to be well fed. A child who hates loud noises does not need field trips to airports, railway stations and construction sites to be well educated. Some people reach adulthood without once being startled by a bulldozer. A child who hates dogs will grow up to be a normal adult who hates dogs. So be it.

Respect for individuality does not mean accepting everything the child does. There are clearly some things about which parents need to take a stand with the child – especially matters of safety. And parents should take stands about a *few* issues of great importance to them. Different parents have different priorities. A friend was absolutely rigid about her children being punctual in getting dressed and ready to leave the house for day care. To her, the worn clothing on the unmade beds, the breakfast spilled on the kitchen floor, and the toys strewn in the living room were unimportant, if only the children were on time. Other mothers may stress the importance of tidiness, even if it takes five minutes longer. Each parent has the right, in my opinion, to exact some compliance from young children on those issues that matter most to the parent. But you cannot make equally high demands on every front at once, or you and the children will lose your minds. Difficult children with low adaptability are especially susceptible to the ill effects of too many parental demands.

If your child despises the car safety seat and screams when she is put in it, too bad. You can either avoid taking her on car trips or listen to her scream for a while, but you cannot take her in the car without the safety seat. Not only is it against the law, but you would be endangering her life, a matter about which you cannot trust her infant judgement. If he rejects all flavours but peanut butter, you may have to find some tasty new recipes for peanut butter–broccoli souffle. Try to find other very popular child-type foods, such as hamburgers, raw celery and carrots, dry cereals, and toasted anything. Even if he will not eat a variety of foods, a balanced diet can be attained with a few redundant choices. You may be sick of looking at peanut butter and celery with Rice Krispies but he may be quite happy and well nourished.

Besides, what are your options? A spoonful of sugar may help the medicine go down, but many parents today disapprove of refined sugar in their children's diets. Many of our parents made us eat what was served on our plates. In our opinion, there is just nothing constructive about forcing hated foods down the child's throat or requiring him to sit at the table until he has cleaned the plate of the green beans and casserole (with its unknown and surely loathsome contents). He'll probably vomit in the plate, and you'll have to clean it up. The next meal will be even more traumatic for both of you, and you can set up a long-term eating problem. At the least, you will have a thrice daily battle over who can make whom do what at the table. Who needs it, if the child can get a proper diet from old standbys?

Bedtime is a nightmare for many parents of difficult children. Such children often have their own interpretations of appropriate day and night activities. A determined two-year-old can outlast you at the late-night film. You have to go to work in the morning. She can go to the childminder and sleep. For parental mental health, the child must fit into some reasonable schedule or be left to entertain herself in the privacy of her cot. Picture books, toys, tape recorders, and other safe objects in her bed may preserve your sanity and her night-owldom at little expense to either party. If she wants company, too, how about going to bed with ear plugs for the several nights it will take to persuade her that you cannot play all night.

In choosing the right care for a difficult child, you need to inform the caregiver fully of your child's idiosyncrasies. If the caregiver cannot accept most, or all, of your child's needs, then find another caregiver. It is not reasonable to expect that the child will suddenly acquire a new personality when he starts day care. Nor is it reasonable to expect that the new caregiver will solve the problems of a difficult child's temperament. Difficult children have more trouble adjusting to any new situation, so that the added burden of adjusting to new expectations of his eating, sleeping, playing and other routines may slow his adjustment to day care to a crawl. A far better adjustment will be possible with a caregiver who understands that children are individuals, some easy and some difficult.

Care outside the home need not have exactly the same requirements and adaptations to the child's characteristics as the home. Caregivers and pre-school teachers are not parents, after all. They have to care for groups of children with some semblance of order and responsibility for the welfare of all of their charges. Teachers and caregivers cannot be partial to any one child but should strive to meet the needs of each child in their care in ways that are compatible with the welfare of the group as a whole. This means that your child is not likely to get *all* the consideration you can give him at home. But there should be as much consideration of his individual needs as is feasible in the small group of babies or pre-school children.

The scope of family responsibility for a child is limitless; there is nothing about the young child's life that is not the business of the family. The parents' role is also diffuse, in that they must provide anything and everything the child needs. Teachers and other caregivers do not have such responsibilities, nor would most parents welcome such intrusions in their legitimate roles. Teachers who become too close to children are often criticized by colleagues and parents as meeting their own needs through their relationships with children in their care.

Affection is an ingredient in all good relationships with babies and young children, but parents have especially intense affectional bonds with their children. Teachers and caregivers have more professional relationships with their young charges. John and Elizabeth Newson (1976), leading psychologists, contrast parent and teacher relationships as follows:

> A good parent-child relationship is in fact very unlike a good teacher-child relationship; yet because the roles have certain *ingredients* in common, though different proportions (nurturance, discipline, information-giving, for example) they are sometimes confused by the participants themselves, to the misunderstanding of all concerned . . . (pp. 401–2).

Parents as teachers

Teachers and caregivers cannot act as parents. What about parents as teachers? In Britain, there is not as much pressure on parents to 'educate' their children in the first three or four years as there is in America. Parents are not usually harangued to begin instructing their children, teaching them to learn the alphabet, count, and recognize letters when they are not yet two. However there is a growth of 'parent education' courses, and of 'home visiting' schemes aimed at families thought to be in need of support – schemes usually directed at teaching mothers how to play with and talk to their children. Many mothers do enjoy these visits. But behind them are two misleading assumptions – that 'instructing' babies early on will give them some advantage, and that professionals know how parents should educate their children. The first is not only misleading but puts unwarranted pressure on parents.

The second assumption is particularly perturbing, as it is often associated with advice that is directed to encourage parents to act like teachers (Tizard and Hughes, 1984). The effort to make parents like teachers is seriously off-target when we recognize that it is *at home* in the comfortable, familiar conversations with Mum that three- and four-year-olds are at their most intellectually adventurous and mature. An exciting study of four-year-olds at home with their mothers in London has turned on its head the view that *school* is where very young children learn. Barbara Tizard and Martin Hughes studied the conversations that girls of four had with their mothers at home, the free-flowing natural exchanges between child and mother while tea was made, lunch was eaten, the washing done, and so on – and those they had at school. What the study revealed was a striking intellectual curiosity on the part of the four-year-olds, evident at home but not at school. When at home they pursued questions that puzzled them, with logic and persistence (How *does* Father Christmas get in if we have no chimney? If a sloping roof is built that way to let the rain drain off, what happens at school where the roof is flat?), and Barbara Tizard and Martin Hughes emphasize that the homes of the children – both middle and working class – provided a very powerful learning environment:

> We found that this learning covered a very wide range of topics, but was especially concerned with the social world. Play, games, stories and even formal 'lessons' provided educational contexts, in the course of which a good deal of general knowledge, as well as early literacy and numeracy skills, were transmitted. But the most frequent learning context was that of

everyday living. Simply by being around their mothers, talking, arguing and endlessly asking questions, the children were being provided with large amounts of information relevant to growing up in our culture. (Tizard and Hughes, 1984, p. 249)

Why did the children show striking intellectual curiosity and power at home with their mothers, rather than at school with their teachers? Barbara Tizard and Martin Hughes comment on a number of reasons, two of particular importance in thinking about the issue of parents-as-teachers. One is the intense affection of the relationship, which allows children to express questions, puzzles and anxieties freely, and which is reflected in the energetic support and close attention that mothers give their children. A second is the shared experience of mother and child:

At home parent and child share a common life, stretching back into the past, and forward into the future. This vast body of shared experience helps the mother to understand what her child is saying, or intending to say. It also facilitates a task essential for intellectual growth – helping the child to make sense of her present experiences by relating them to past experiences, as well as to her existing framework of knowledge. (Tizard and Hughes, 1984, p. 250)

While Barbara Tizard and Martin Hughes emphasize the richness and value of the learning that can take place at home, they stress that children learn other things in other contexts, and that their results do not imply that a mother who works will be depriving her child of crucial learning experiences:

Moreover, we have no reason to suppose that the process of education through one-to-one dialogue that we have described needs to take place all day and every day. It may be that one episode of real concentration on a child each day, or one question seriously answered, is as valuable as hours of less focused attention. In any case we do not believe that parents must always answer their children's questions, and constantly engage in long conversations with them. Children have to learn that adults have other concerns, and cannot be constantly available to them . . . (Tizard and Hughes, 1984, p. 260).

In our view, any pressure on parents to be teachers of their babies and young children is quite unnecessary and doesn't help them. It can even hinder them. One does not have to object to specific instructional programmes; one only has to ask what parents are giving up by so structuring their interactions with their baby. When father is counting blocks with twelve-month-old Jimmy, wouldn't he be more important in his son's life if he was focusing on Jimmy rather than on counting? Parents who delight in the silly and funny surprises of everyday life with their children have, we believe, happier relationships with them than deadly serious instructors do. And as Barbara Tizard and Martin Hughes have shown, it is the relaxed conversations between children and their parents that are in any case likely to be particularly fruitful for their intellectual development.

Why infant instruction?

What's the point of infant instruction, anyway? There is nothing you can teach your baby by dint of great effort that she will not learn naturally without any instruction in a few months. With pre-school children, intense instruction in reading skills may accelerate the acquisition of reading by a few years, but at ten the accelerated child will not read more fluently or with more comprehension than a similarly bright child who learned to read at six or seven. Meanwhile, the parents have spent much of their time with the child teaching it to read, rather than interacting in other ways. There are costs to parents in being teachers rather than parents.

Babies learn most of what they know from interactions with their parents, but not of the formal, instructional variety. Babies learn from spontaneous, everyday events – the postman at the door with a package to open, the dog next door chasing a cat, sugar dissolving in warm water, a train ride – all of which need adult interpretation. They are real events of interest and concern to babies and young children. Picture books focus on babies' real-life experiences for the same good reasons. By contrast, infant education is artificial and out of context. How can you explain to a twelve-month-old why he should concentrate on the distinctions between upper- and lower-case letters?

Older pre-school children do benefit from some formal instruction, because three- and four-year-olds have minds that transcend their own immediate experiences. They can learn from other people's ideas and images. They are the most enthusiastic Superman and astronaut fans. Fantasy flights, vicarious safaris, and building castles are pre-school delights. That is why nursery schools are so justifiedly popular.

The research that is alleged to support the importance of early instruction has been grossly misunderstood by the advocates of teach-your-baby-early. Let us illustrate with a parable in statistics.

Did you know that when the birth rate goes up, more coffee beans are imported into the United States? This is a true association. Let us try to explain why the popularities of babies and coffee beans rise and fall together. First, it could be that coffee keeps potential parents awake at night, after which they retire to bed to make babies (coffee causes babies). Second, it could be that having babies makes parents stay up more at night and drink more coffee (babies cause coffee). Third, perhaps there is no causal link between babies and coffee at all. Maybe their fates rise and fall according to the action of some other cause. Maybe babies and coffee merely co-occur. The world is full of co-occurrences, which are often called correlations.

If we leap from co-occurrences to causal statements, we are likely to fall into a logical chasm. There are often other factors that cause the correlation of such events. The correlation of coffee and babies is just such an example. When the economy is booming, people have more babies, buy more coffee, clothing, automobiles, televisions, and so forth. In a recession, people are more likely to postpone childbearing and to give up the luxury of coffee. The correlation between babies and coffee results from a much larger economic cause.

In the same vein, you know that bright parents tend to have, on the average, bright children. Bright parents also tend to provide more stimulating interactions for their children. Bright parents have more conversations with their young children than less bright parents. Less competent parents are more likely to ignore their children's questions and comments. Ergo, illogicians conclude that the ways that parents interact with their young children *cause* the children to be intellectually brighter or duller.

The baby-stimulators have misinterpreted a *correlation* between intense instruction and good development as a *causal* connection. Just because we all observe that intelligent parents both have bright children and interact with them in stimulating ways, we have no right to conclude that the interaction causes the child to be bright. We could just as well conclude that bright children evoke stimulating interactions from their parents by being alert, interested, and fun to talk to. We could also conclude that the correlation between parents' interactions and children's intelligence is caused primarily by a third factor – such as genetic transmission of high and low intelligence from parents to children, leading to interesting or dull interactions between them.

Less bright parents have less bright children in part for genetic reasons: intelligence is transmitted by parents to their children as potential development, coded in the genes. With a normally stimulating environment, children of bright parents will most often develop above-average intelligence. With the same normally stimulating environment, children of less bright parents will, on average, develop lower IQs. Even within the same family, however, sisters and brothers differ substantially in IQ scores, because each gets a different combination of genes. So don't expect all of your children to become geniuses, no matter who you are or what you do. Although there is a *correlation* between parents' intelligence and the kind of rearing environment they provide for their children, we cannot conclude that such interactions will make all children bright.

In fact, studies of adoptive families show that what children gained from intellectual stimulation in their families depended more on their ability to learn than on the intensity of the instruction the parents provided. Adopted children profited from the good environments of adoptive homes, but how high their IQ scores were depended more on their genetic background than on the particular educational practices of the adoptive parents (Scarr and Weinberg, 1983; Scarr and McCartney, 1983). Families who spent more time in educational activities with their adopted children did not have any brighter adolescents than families with more casual attitudes toward teaching. But adopted children with bright natural parents who gave them up for adoption at birth turned out to be brighter than adopted children with less intelligent natural parents, regardless of which kind of adoptive home they grew up in.

The message from this tangent on correlations, causation and adoptive families is that there is no evidence that parents need to be deliberate teachers of their children. Just by being themselves and interacting with their children in perfectly normal ways, parents provide the world that suits the development of any normal baby. Unless your child has special needs, such as physical, mental or emotional handicaps, just being with you is enough. There is no evidence that doing elaborate instructional activities with babies and young children has *any* effect on their intellectual development in the long run. Once again, Edward Zigler sums it up:

> Parents must also be helped to recognize that their child's development is not entirely in their own hands to shape, but that the child is endowed by nature with individuality and unique potential. One *can* provide a child with experiences conducive to his or her full intellectual growth. But parents must be clearly aware that there are individual differences between children, even between children in the same family, and that the impact of a child's experiences is determined in large part by the child's own nature (Zigler and Cascione, 1980, p. 83).

Good child care depends on parents' and caregivers' knowledge of child development, their understanding of each child's unique personality and abilities, and their willingness to provide care that is appropriate for the child's stage of development and individually tailored to the child. So be informed and be yourself. Enjoy time with your child, whether you are laughing or interpreting an interesting event. Why else would you want to be a parent?

PART FOUR
Other Care

CHAPTER EIGHT

Who's Afraid of Day Care?

The idea that babies and young children can be successfully reared apart from their parents both horrifies and fascinates parents in Britain. We have been taught that parental – indeed, maternal – care is essential for children's emotional health. Communal or institutional child rearing is the antithesis of middle-class beliefs about children and parenting.

Yet most parents have a guilty fascination with the idea that they could escape much of the mind-numbing drudgery of child care and still assure their baby's optimum development. Somehow, wealthy families can get away with child rearing by maids, nannies and governesses, but middle-class parents are supposed to provide all child care themselves. Most parents cannot aspire to a nanny, but they can imagine a community that provides child care for working parents, even a community that takes over the majority of the child's care. But a major shift in the child's care from parents to others – even while they work – makes many parents very nervous indeed.

Institutional Care Versus Day Care

Arguments against child care outside the family are too often made as though the choices are all or nothing. Once the dam of total parental care is broken, the child will be swept from her parents' arms into the limbo of an impersonal institution. There are two distortions in this image: working parents use part-time child care – they do not abandon their babies – and day care is not institutionalization.

Comparisons of babies and children in institutions to those in day care have frightened many parents. Institutionalized children, abandoned or taken away from their parents, are at the mercy of caregivers who may be impersonal and who may change so often that the babies cannot become familiar with even a few to whom they can become attached. Children who grow up in families but spend time away from home every day have a totally different experience, because they have consistent relationships and daily experience with their parents as well as with day caregivers. Yet some experts have compared institutionalized infants to others in day care. Such unfortunates have been used as examples of what can happen if babies are deprived of full-time maternal care. Those who make such comparisons confuse poor quality care with part-time mothering.

To disentangle the effects of part-time mothering from the effects of poor quality care, let us consider the more appropriate examples of high quality, nonmaternal care – children reared in communal settings. How do they fare? Communally reared children are rare in Britain, but there have been examples here and elsewhere of communities that, for ideological reasons, relieved mothers of the primary care of their children. In the next chapter, we will consider realistic alternative forms of day care, their advantages and disadvantages for children of different ages and temperaments. In this chapter, we will look at an extreme form of nonmaternal care and its effects on children. Is it harmful to put one's baby or young child into a communal setting where the primary care responsibility is handed over to others, even if they provide loving, stimulating care?

Nobody's children

From the 1850s, British children whose families could not care for them were often placed in institutions called orphanages or children's homes. At the time, the caretakers in children's institutions considered their major job to be keeping their little charges clean, fed and Godly. Infants by the hundreds of thousands in the western world were placed in orphanages to pine away for lack of human contact. Dozens of cots lined the walls of dozens of rooms. In each cot was a lonely baby staring vacantly at a white ceiling. Some of the better institutions decided to increase cleanliness by draping the cot walls with white sheets, further depriving the babies of visual experience. The children were rarely handled or played with, and they developed in predictably retarded ways.

As we have stressed throughout the book, infants need contact with and stimulation by familiar adults who interact in loving ways. Michael Rutter (1982b) summarized the literature on 'maternal' deprivation by concluding, as we do, that it was deprivation of human contact, not of a mother *per se*, that caused such poor emotional, motor and mental development of institutionalized infants.

None the less, proponents of exclusive maternal care used the research on institutionalized infants to scare mothers into staying at home full time with their babies. Despite much research to the contrary, the scare lingers on in the minds of those who do not (or do not want to) understand the difference between full-time institutional care of infants by unstimulating caregivers and day care in a friendly home or communal setting when the child also has devoted parents.

Custodial care

Custodial care has some of the flavour of institutions. It implies that the child is merely tended physically and not really stimulated or loved. Some day-care settings in Britain are custodial, especially when there are too many babies and toddlers for one caretaker to manage in any other way. Can you imagine trying to provide individualized attention for twelve babies and toddlers under two? Imagine having to cook their lunches, hold them for bottles, and change their nappies. No time could be given to talking, singing and playing baby games with them.

In situations where custodial care is the only affordable or available option, the child is bored for much of the day, not playing, not learning anything about people or about the physical world – a great waste of the baby's valuable time. The children in custodial care are deprived of daytime stimulation, but they do have parents who pick them up after work and who spend time with them during evenings, weekends and holidays. Today's babies should not have mere custodial care, and it is a national disgrace that we do not support developmentally appropriate care for all our children. But even children in custodial care are not institutionalized as in the old days.

Children of the Community

Many times in the last two centuries, idealistic groups have hit upon the idea that children need not belong exclusively to their biological parents. Such groups hoped that children reared communally by loving caregivers who were not the parents would have fewer personality problems than children reared primarily by their parents. Parents, too, were thought to benefit from sharing their child-rearing chores with the community. Thus, communal child rearing was invented independently many times.

Several lasting communal experiments arose from European political upheavals in the nineteenth century, such as the Hutterians, the Bruderhof and the Amana community. After the First World War, other ideological communities appeared: many were short lived but several are still successful. Good examples of success in communal living are the kibbutzim, established in Palestine in the early part of this century, and the Bruderhof in the Eastern United States. In the social revolution of the 1960s and early 1970s, young adults formed communities in Britain and the United States, some of which were casual collections of pot-smokers but others of which were serious replicas of the older, ideologically motivated communities. One such replica is Twin Oaks in Virginia (Komar, 1983).

Because of the traditional emphasis on mother-child relationships in early life, research on communally reared children is particularly relevant to the debate about the mother's importance as a special caregiver. Freudians predicted that communally reared children would be emotionally impoverished. The failure to have an exclusive attachment to one's mother, or at least intense relationships with one's parents, should result in shallow feelings for others. At worst, such children should not trust others. At best, they should be emotionally bland and uncaring.

The 'maternal deprivation' of communally reared children was supposed to result in more mental illness, more immature emotional development, poorer identification with parents, and too great a reliance on peers (Beit-Hallahmi and Rabin, 1977). Communal rearing, however loving the care, was presumed to put children at risk – somewhere between the fortunate youngsters of traditional families with two parents including a full-time mother, and pitiful orphans (Goldfarb, 1943, 1955; Spitz, 1945).

Freeing parents and children

One of the major ways Utopian communities establish their ideals is to dilute the rights and responsibilities of individual parents for their children. Sharing child-rearing responsibilities is meant to free women from the bonds of conventional families. Women are to be economically independent of their husbands and free of continuous child care. Children are also to be freed from the emotional bonds of the nuclear family by sharing in the love of the larger community.

Because membership is voluntary, all members of the community can be counted on to share the beliefs of the group in shared lives. Parents in communities who share their childrens' care do not feel that they are neglectful, nor are they. Children in idealistic communities are well cared for, in keeping with their importance as the future generation. Their care is just not carried out primarily by their parents or by any one person during all their growing-up years. Nor do the children feel neglected, because parents' and children's interpretations of their rearing depend on the meaning that the community gives it.

How children feel about being with their parents a few hours a day and residing in a children's house in an intentional community is bound to be different from the feelings of children in ordinary society who are, for example, in foster care because their parents cannot cope with the demands of child rearing. Foster children's own parents have failed as parents. Even if foster families provide love and good care, children know their real parents are inadequate. The meaning that ordinary society gives to this situation is entirely different from the shared child rearing of intentional communities, and foster children suffer accordingly.

Children of the kibbutz

We will now take a closer look at communal child rearing, beginning with the many studies of kibbutzim, the successful communes of Israel. Collective settlements in Palestine began in 1910 and flowered with waves of immigration from Europe from the 1920s on. Kibbutzim are not merely economic arrangements to make the deserts bloom. Rather, kibbutzim strive to embody the ideals of economic collectivism and social equality of men and women. Men and women therefore rotate jobs, including those usually assigned exclusively to men or to women in Europe and the United States.

To free women from exclusive responsibility for rearing children, the kibbutzim established children's houses with professional caregivers. Fathers are expected to participate as parents to the same extent that mothers do. Founders of the kibbutz movement were intent 'on the dismantling of the traditional, bourgeois family, with its close mother–child ties, which was perceived as promoting selfishness and individualism' (Beit-Hallahmi and Rabin, 1977, p. 533). Although they have not achieved all of their ideals – indeed, in the last ten years they have reversed many of their earlier socialist ideals – the kibbutzim are a successful demonstration of communal child rearing (Beit-Hallahmi and Rabin, 1977).

The typical kibbutz has about 500 residents, including children and some youth groups in training. Some have as many as 2,000 residents. They operate as a village with considerable democracy. All members take their turns in the central kitchen and dining room. The eating facilities are the centre of kibbutz communal life, because families do not prepare their own meals. Adults eat together three times a day. Children often eat separately in their own 'children's houses'.

The family life of the kibbutz is very different from that of European and American families. Families are not economic units, and they do not have exclusive responsibility for the socialization and control of their children. This results from a principle of kibbutz life: the liberation of women and children from the subjugation of the traditional family, which the founders viewed with profound dissatisfaction (Beit-Hallahmi and Rabin, 1977). Children's emotional enslavement by exclusive parents and women's enslavement in the home were to be undone by the formation of egalitarian communities with shared child rearing.

In the earliest months of a baby's life, the mother typically spends a great deal of time with her child in the infant house. She is encouraged to breast-feed on demand, so during the first six weeks of the infant's life she must be available. Even mothers who do not breast-feed take full care of their babies in the first six weeks, because they are not expected to return to work until after that period.

From the time the baby is about six weeks old until he is four months old, the mother returns to work about halftime, but she is available for about four hours a day to feed, change and play with the baby. At night he is cared for by the infant group's nurse. From this time until the end of the first year, mothers continue to be involved in their baby's daily care, but the nurse and her assistant, who are assigned to a regular group of four to six infants, are expected to comfort them, care for their physical health, and keep track of any problems.

In the traditional kibbutzim, parents are with their babies for about two hours in the late afternoon, usually in their own rooms. Any siblings will also be there to play with the baby. Parents can give their children undivided attention during these family times, because these hours are not taken up with household chores. Kibbutz parents spend about as much time in direct interactions with their children as do typical British parents, who must also attend to food preparation, laundry, cleaning, and the like.

The infant house keeps children until they are about fifteen months old, when they are transferred as a group to the toddler house. Their infant nurse moves with them and stays with them for the next three years. The toddler house has many play facilities, bedrooms for four to six children per room, and a dining facility. In the toddler house, the nurse assumes primary responsibility for her charges; parents take less and less responsibility for their children, although they continue to take their children home each day. The nurse toilet trains and teaches self-feeding, dressing, and other toddler social skills. In most kibbutzim, parents put their children to bed in the toddler house at night; in others the regular nurse does. The toddler house has a night watchwoman, who makes sure everyone is safe and tries to comfort those who wake in the night.

At about five years of age, children from three toddler groups are combined into an eighteen-child kindergarten group that will remain together for the next two or three years. Two nurse-teachers now conduct the daily routine, which includes some formal group instruction as well as individual activities. The kindergarten is housed in a separate building, which has bedrooms for four or five youngsters each, play facilities, small gardens, and enclosures for pets. The nurses are now clearly the dominant socializing figures in the children's lives.

Throughout the children's growing-up years, they join their parents at home for daily visits. Most parents also establish a corner or cupboard in their rooms for each child to keep a few belongings, even though most of their toys and clothes are in their own rooms at the children's houses. According to Rabin (1965), parents begin to complain that their children are more interested in their peer group than in family activities at about the same time that parents here sense the transition – at about seven to eight years old.

At seven, a permanent group is formed for the next eleven years, or until the children graduate from secondary school. The children live together in bedrooms for three or four youngsters, meet in discussion, study together, celebrate birthdays, and build a cooperative society that works, sleeps, eats and plays together. Often the children have a miniature farm with fields and animals for which they are responsible. Coeducational groups continue to live together through adolescence, which shocks the parents of college-age students in the 1980s far less than it did parents of the 1950s.

Parents of older children and adolescents generally show interest in them, spend time with them daily and at major holidays. Except for the intense mother–infant contact of the breastfeeding period, fathers have the same pattern of contact with their children as mothers – after work and on rest days. Parental power is diluted, however, by the fact that children live with a steady group of peers under the supervision of nurses and teachers.

To summarize the psychological qualities of communal rearing in the kibbutz, Beit-Hallahmi and Rabin (1977) offer the following:

The number of significant others interacting with the child is higher than in the traditional family, but the relationships with some of these figures are nonexclusive and discontinuous. The *metapelet* (caretaker) takes care of a group of children and is likely to be changed several times during childhood. In the infants' and children's group, the child is exposed to a uniform, less personal treatment, and his needs are satisfied less readily than in the traditional family. We might say that the child in the kibbutz lives in two worlds: One is the family unit where he spends some of his time in continuous, exclusive and personalized interaction, and the other is the children's house, where interaction with adults is discontinuous, non-exclusive and less personal . . .

What is most important from a psychological point of view is the presence of multiple caretakers at an early stage in the children's development. This characteristic, and especially the limited contact with the mother, has raised several questions regarding its possible effects. Should the multiple caretaking be regarded as a form of maternal deprivation, maternal substitution, or multiple mothering? On the basis of available research . . . we may conclude that the latter formulation is correct (p. 534).

Social science looks at the kibbutz

In the heyday of psychoanalysis, experts were close to hysterics over communal child rearing. Theoretically, being reared by several adults, however loving, *must* be a disaster for personality development. Several experts actually went to Israel briefly to 'observe'. Disaster was in the eyes of the beholders, and they were shocked at what they saw (for example, Bettelheim, 1969).

Observers who believe in exclusive mothering and the importance of early experience noted signs of maternal deprivation among the infants and young children. Infants were said to be listless. Young children were said to have excessive thumbsucking, bedwetting, and aggressive behaviour. Older children were characterized as introverted, insolent, hostile and insecure (Spiro, 1958), and as egocentric and envious, with little capacity for affective relationships, a good deal of mistrust, and considerable mutual contempt (Kardiner, 1954). None of these conclusions was based on a systematic study of communal rearing or its products.

Yet other observers, less committed to psychoanalysis, noted that the allegedly disturbed emotional life of the pre-school years (the lack of exclusive mothering) did not seem to leave its mark on the stability of adolescents or adults (Caplan, 1954; Irvine, 1952). Their conclusions deviated from those who believed that early experience determines later personality.

In 1953 a conference was held to consider the threats to children of communal child rearing. The reported impressions of infant listlessness and toddler disturbance, attributed to the early years of maternal deprivation, fitted into the theoretical framework; the observations of well-adjusted older kibbutzniks did not (Rabin, 1965). The experts debated two questions about communal rearing, both loaded with psychoanalytic preconceptions:

1. Are children's personalities 'homogenized' by communal rearing? Is there a loss of individuality?
2. Can older kibbutz-reared children and adults *really* be considered emotionally mature?

Psychologists with Victorian ideas were puzzled about the lack of evidence for what should have been disastrous outcomes for the children of the kibbutz. Comparisons were made between orphans in impersonal institutions and commune children, because neither had exclusive mothers. Other characteristics of institutions, such as the lack of sensory or intellectual stimulation of any kind and the impersonal care, did not strike many of the experts as important differences between orphanages and communal situations. Kibbutz children were clearly loved and cherished by the community, but this seemed to escape notice.

Later studies gave the lie to the earlier unsystematic 'observations'. Kaffman (1965) studied 403 kibbutz-reared children, including *all* children from ages one to twelve in three kibbutzim. He compared the incidence of disturbed behaviour, including thumb-sucking, bedwetting, and aggressive behaviour, between the kibbutzniks and larger samples of American children. He found no differences in the frequencies of childhood disturbances, with the exception of oral behaviours. Kibbutz children persisted in thumb-sucking longer than American children but had significantly fewer eating disturbances. Rabin (1965) explains that adults in kibbutzim are tolerant of thumb-sucking in older children, so that there is little pressure on them to stop. Nothing much was made of the eating disturbances of mother-reared American children.

Caplan (1954) reported that there were no more personality disturbances among the older kibbutz children than in comparable American samples and that young adults were remarkably non-neurotic. Rabin's more extensive testing and observations support that conclusion. Rabin (1965, 1971; Rabin and Beit-Hallahmi, 1982) studied eight traditional kibbutzim. His research covered the intellectual and personality development of infants, children, adolescents and young adults, and employed the conventional measures of western society. For infants, a developmental mental scale and a social maturity scale were used; for children, adolescents and young adults, several projective measures and observations of adult-child interactions were used.

Rabin compared the kibbutz-reared children with those in four Israeli agricultural villages where parents reared their own children but cooperated in economic production. Thus, many environmental conditions, such as urban versus rural settings and Israeli versus U S communities, that could have affected the results did not. He found that kibbutz youngsters grow up to be fine adults, just as well-adjusted and intelligent as Israeli children reared by traditional families.

More recent research (Bar-Tal, Raviv and Shavit, 1981) confirms the age-appropriate development of kibbutz children at nursery school and early school age. Compared with children reared in conventional families, communally reared children are no more and no less helpful to others, and children in both rearing groups attribute their attitudes equally to their parents. In other studies, kibbutz children have scored better than conventionally reared children on measures of social responsibility and moral reasoning.

All in all, the communally reared children of Israel are far from the emotional disasters that psychoanalytic theory predicted. Neither have they been saved from all personality problems, as the founders of the kibbutz movement had hoped when they freed children from their parents. In any reasonable environment, children seem to grow up to be themselves. There is no evidence that communal rearing with stimulating, caring adults is either the ruination or the salvation of children.

'The joyful community'

One of the first things that the Bruderhof did when its founders established the first community in 1920 was to pool all wealth and property, according to the example of the first Christians. Its members have lived by this principle ever since. Three Bruderhof ('place of brothers') communities in the Northeastern United States have thrived on the production of high-quality wooden toys, sold mainly to schools. Members are mostly college-educated, middle-class Christians, who have chosen to live communally and to rear their children collectively. Even if one is reared in the community, one has to gain brotherhood as an adult through the religious and personal conviction that the Bruderhof is the chosen way of life. The majority of children reared in 'the joyful community' return after being educated through college.

Communal sharing in the Bruderhof is more than an economic arrangement, as in the kibbutzim. Members work together, eat together, meet almost every night, raise their children together, and spend their entire lives together (Zablocki, 1971). Communal child rearing is only one, but an essential, part of the entire shared life of the Bruderhof.

Men and women marry for life; no divorce or remarriage is allowed. Married couples are expected to produce as many children as God permits, so that families are often large. The birth of a new baby is an occasion for rejoicing. Both of the new parents spend the first six weeks of the baby's life living with him in the Mother House, while someone in the community takes full charge of their older children. When the baby is six weeks old, the parents go home and the infant moves to the Baby House. The mother returns to work almost full time, although she is allowed time to visit the Baby House to breast-feed her infant. If the baby gets hungry while she is at work, the caregivers will call her to come and feed him.

Babies are cared for by a nurse in groups of four until they are about a year old. In the second to fourth years of life, there is a nurse for every eight children. The Baby House is well equipped with bedrooms, play space, and rooms where parents can visit their youngsters. Babies and children are put to bed by their parents but spend nearly all their waking hours being looked after by other community members.

At four the children move to the Pre-school House for the two years until they enter elementary school. At all times and at all ages, the children are in close contact with their parents and other adults in the community. A child who is not doing well or is breaking the rules of the community is given a residence with someone who will provide proper training and example. He or she may be allowed little contact with other children or parents until the penance is done. The community is strict and loving to all its children.

At adolescence the Bruderhof children enter the local high schools, which represent quite a change from the sheltered lives they have led. Most seem to adapt to the experience and to emerge as better-than-average students. Most go on to college, although some re-enter the community at eighteen. The experience of growing up in the community is not seen as traumatic; for three generations, the grown-up children have returned to live there. 75 per cent of the children reared in the Bruderhof choose to stay in the community and to rear their own children there.

According to Zablocki, the children grow up well. They are loving adults with few problems about their childhoods.

> The Bruderhof child's life is full and happy despite lack of contact with the outside world. Every sabra (adult who was reared in the community from childhood) that I spoke with remembered his or her (pre-teenage) childhood with pleasure: 'Actually I think the community is very good for children. . . . You're with your age group all the time. You're away from your parents except for at night. You're not constantly with your mother . . .'

These brief accounts of two intentional communities illustrate the principles of many others. Children reared communally need not suffer either temporary or permanent damage. The idea that mothers should be the exclusive or even primary caregivers for their children is not universally shared. When a community believes otherwise, children seem to grow up as well as they do in traditional families, as we define them.

Good Child Rearing is Just That

There are many similarities in the rearing of children in intentional communities, because they share child care and they value their children. The care they provide is probably no better or worse in the abstract than care in nuclear families where the mother provides most child care. Communities such as the kibbutzim and the Bruderhof do a good job with their children, just as many nuclear families do. There are far more similarities in the children's outcomes as adults than there are differences, which is just as well for society. That gives us options for child rearing, once we work out how sharing responsibilities for child rearing can fit into late-twentieth-century life in Britain.

With the majority of women with young children now in the labour force, and 75 per cent of them predicted to be there by 1990, it is perhaps time that we consider alternatives. The major intention of this brief review of communal rearing is to suggest that good child care can be compatible with working mothers. Daytime care by loving adults other than parents is not the threat to their emotional development once proposed. Even residence in children's houses does not disrupt children's stability, when the parents and the community agree on the arrangement.

We do not advocate day care or communal rearing *per se*. Child care must fit the pattern of work and family life approved by the parents and by the larger social group to which they belong. We suggest, however, that we can think more broadly of alternatives when we know they need not be harmful to children.

CHAPTER NINE

Childminders, Day Nurseries and Babysitters

Where Are Our Children?

In Britain, most babies and pre-school children with working mothers are cared for in homes – their own or others'. According to a recent national survey, about 65 per cent of the under-fives whose mothers work full time are looked after by relatives (44 per cent by grandmothers, 13 per cent by fathers). 23 per cent are cared for by childminders, 6 per cent by babysitters and 3 per cent in exchanges with friends. 9 per cent are in day nurseries. Of the children whose mothers work part time, an even higher percentage is looked after by family members (The Report of the 1980 Department of Employment/Office of Population Censuses and Surveys *Women and Employment Survey*, Martin and Roberts, 1984). A tiny proportion of the children whose mothers work, then, are provided for by 'statutory', government-supported arrangements. With so little government provision, and with no tax concessions for the costs of child care, it is not surprising that studies of mothers who work show that these women very frequently have to make complicated arrangements with relatives or friends, have to settle for unsatisfactory but just-affordable care, or have to work unsocial hours. 77 per cent of women on evening shift work, and 69 per cent of part-time nightworkers, for instance, have young children. In families in which the children are looked after by their fathers, this is *not* primarily because their fathers are unemployed or on shift work. Rather, the mothers in these families are particularly likely to be working unsocial hours (Osborn, Butler and Morris, 1984). In such homes one imagines that as one parent goes to bed, the other leaves for work, and they meet occasionally at the breakfast table.

We don't know much about the nature of this care by relatives, beyond the difficulty that it poses for husbands and wives to have any family life together. Research is underway, but there is for the moment no documentation of how economic and social stresses are influencing, for instance, the availability of 'grandmother care'. It seems very likely that the same conditions that are forcing single mothers to go to work are forcing more and more 'young' grandmothers to stay employed.

Our country has enormous problems with the care of young children with working parents. Why is the provision of adequate child care such a difficult problem, when other countries provide care for the next generation? Questions of quantity, quality and kinds of care raise different issues.

First, let us consider quantity of care. It is a problem that is becoming increasingly acute. The proportion of pre-school children cared for in day nurseries has declined from 17 per cent in 1948 (Douglas and Blomfield, 1958, p. 123) to 6 per cent in 1965 (Hunt, 1968, p. 94) and to 3 per cent in 1984 (Osborn, Butler and Morris, 1984). Yet in this period, as we've seen, the number of working mothers had dramatically increased, as has the number of single parents whose children cannot be left at home in the care of a spouse. By the time that they reach school age, many children receive no child care outside school hours, even though their mothers work. According to the OPCS survey, in 1980 30 per cent of full-time and 53 per cent of part-time women workers with a youngest child aged five to ten years made no child-care arrangements (Martin and Roberts, 1984). While some of these mothers were only working during school hours, it is very likely that quite a high proportion of the children were left alone for long periods. And while we have no reliable detailed figures on the numbers of pre-school children who are left on their own, the OPCS survey shows that no child-care arrangements are made for the pre-school children of 7 per cent of full-time and 17 per cent of part-time working mothers. Very similar figures are estimated for the US: about 7 per cent of pre-school children in America are left on their own for at least part of the time that their parents work. Of the eight million pre-school children with working parents in America this means that more than half a million are left alone for part or all of the day. Some of us would call both the British and American situations national scandals.

Second, the quality of care available raises other issues. Even if enough places for pre-school children could be provided privately, many parents could not afford to pay for the kind of care that is good for little children. Good care means only a few babies and toddlers per caregiver, whose salary must then be provided, if not by government support, by only a few working parents. Good care also means a cheerful, stimulating and safe physical environment, which costs more money than a dank basement in a firetrap building.

One could imagine the establishment of affordable nurseries to accommodate children while their parents work. These nurseries could charge less than other forms of child care by skimping on the number and quality of the caregivers, the toys and play facilities, the buildings and the food. The babies would merely exist for nine hours a day, five days a week.

Some day-care centres in America, especially in low-income areas, approach this nightmare. Although most states have laws about minimal standards of physical care, the babies and young children are merely kept safe, clean and fed. No attempts are made to provide them with loving attention or stimulation. But then, what can adults do in such a setting when they have two or three times too many children to care for? The only way for some centres to be economically viable is to make every paid caregiver the 'mother' of octuplet babies.

Third, types of care that are appropriate for older children are not suitable for younger babies. Although it suits most four-year-olds to be in a group of eight, babies under twelve months cannot thrive in such numbers. Yet many working mothers cannot possibly afford to support more than a small proportion of a caregiver's wage and the other costs of child care. Woe to the working mother with two pre-school children!

The appropriate kinds of child-care provision for young children ought to be judged by what is important for the child's development. Under-threes need close attention from adults, who coo responsively to the four-month-olds, name objects for the twelve-month-olds and have conversations about zoo animals with the four-year-olds. Hugs and smiles are needed by all young children – and indeed by all of us.

Over-threes need adults as well. But they also enjoy and profit from time and friendship with other children and from more formal instruction. They are more curious about the world than are younger children, ready to explore larger territory, ask more questions, and learn more from experiences outside the home or nursery setting. They like trips to see the local fire-engines, building sites, and zoos. They are more interested in the exciting world outside the family than are under-threes, whose major needs are well fulfilled by smaller spaces and smaller events.

Pre-school children – threes to fives – *talk* to other children. Their conversations may seem a little odd to adults because they don't follow all the rules of adult discourse. They interrupt, fail to follow the topic of discussion over several turns of the talk, and carry on extensive monologues despite their companions' lack of interest. But their relationships with the other children that they meet become more and more important – to them, and to the way in which they develop.

Three- and four-year-olds can also listen for minutes at a time to a teacher reading a story or demonstrating how to make pottery. Younger children find such concentration difficult. Under-threes are more attuned to sitting in an adult's lap and being read a brief story, or to being taken on a trip to the local shops. It is obvious, but cannot be stressed enough: we must consider how child care is best organized for each child's level of social, emotional and intellectual development.

Another message that this book has stressed is that children are very different from one another in ways that should influence choices about child care. Some children are relatively shy and need close contact with a few adults. Some children are mature for their years and are ready for experiences that others of their age would find alarming, or mystifying. Other children are developmentally less mature than their peers and need care that is more typical for children who are younger. Just as some children are physically smaller than others, some are socially and emotionally more vulnerable. We don't shout 'Grow up!' at a short child; why should we yell at a slow-grower for his pattern of emotional development? If we have any choice about kinds of care, then it's important to think hard about each child as a person before deciding what will suit him best at what age and stage.

And do not fear that the best child-care arrangements are necessarily the most expensive. The best childminders look after children because they *like* children. They could earn much more by cleaning offices or working at the local supermarket. The fact that childminders and nursery nurses (indeed, most traditional women's jobs) are so miserably paid raises an ideological conflict for other working mothers, one that is not resolvable by individual mothers. To join the exploiters of those who care for children seems hypocritical, but what does our society offer as options? Being unemployed is about the only option to exploiting other women as caregivers. And that is not an option for most women who work.

Some Child Care Considerations

Suppose a child is sent to a minder or nursery where things don't go well for him: what does it mean for his future? Children are not as fragile as some experts would have us believe. Nor are the experiences of the first few years of life as important to later development as some earlier psychologists believed. Young children are resilient people that evolution has adapted to many circumstances. But children deserve to be happy – even if no long-term trouble ensues from a less-than-happy experience. And the quality of care and education that a child receives matters *whatever* their age. Although early childhood is so plastic, good experiences can have lasting impact and can obliterate earlier effects. We want to be able to give our children the best care – and parents' comfort about their choice of child care may be as important for children as the specifics of the care. Sally Provence (1982) argues that the key to child care that works well is the collaboration between parents and those providing the care to create a consistent and agreeable world for the child.

For most working mothers in Britain there is very little choice about the kind of care they can arrange for their child. Childminding, or a babysitter in your own home, are probably the only ways that you can arrange regular provision for the whole working day. But it is important, nevertheless, to be aware of the kinds of differences there may be *within* these settings. And for those who do have the money and opportunity to decide between a babysitter, a childminder or a nursery setting, how do you decide which will best suit your child?

Babysitters in your home

Children at home alone with a babysitter have the security of remaining in their own familiar environment, and the opportunity for one-to-one attention from a single caregiver. Sitters vary widely in their responsiveness to children and in the continuity of care that they provide. There is of course no responsible person to note what in fact happens during the day. No one is the wiser if the sitter spends the day watching soap operas on TV. If she presents you with a happy, cheerful baby at the end of the day, things can't be too bad. But you won't know if the baby in fact spent most of the day in her cot. Sitters or nannies in the home are also usually the most expensive form of child care. We have both personally employed sitters in our homes for some of our children, when they were babies or pre-school children. In general our experiences were mediocre to good. The children liked some, were less keen on others. Only one was what we would consider a superb caregiver. Incidentally, she was a mother of school-aged children, without any special training, but with great warmth, sympathy and good humour, and an intelligent concern for the children's interests and their individual personalities.

There was one nightmare, however, for one of us, as Sandra Scarr relates:

One afternoon I returned home to find my third child, then a talkative and delightful eighteen-month-old, crying. The sitter ran out of the door as fast as she could leave. Before I could ask what had happened, she was gone. Rebecca said, 'Kathy hit me! Kathy hit me!' I soothed her and took her upstairs for a bath. Upon undressing her, I could see large red welts forming on her bottom and thighs. The sitter had beaten her badly.

I called the police, who came immediately and took my complaint. They examined the baby with sensitivity and photographed her growing bruises. Unfortunately, they said, there was nothing they could do without a witness. Eighteen-month-olds are not suitable witnesses, it seems. Yes, they knew about this young woman, a practical nurse by training. Two other families had filed complaints about her for child abuse. The police were powerless to prosecute, however. They were not even allowed to tell parents about the other complaints, because the allegations were unproven; they just wanted me to know that I was not the first parent to have a child beaten by this woman.

Kathy had worked for so many families that she managed to give references to parents whose children she had not beaten, and to be employed yet another time. In retrospect, the reasons she gave for leaving her earlier employ seemed false: to get married (when I employed her she said she was divorced), to take care of her ageing grandmother who later died (who knows?), and to take a better-paying job (perhaps). Kathy was an experience I will never forget. No one was there to prevent the abuse or to testify about it. We were all powerless to prevent an almost certain recurrence. The lack of supervision and public examination of what can go on in the home is a major problem, in my view – one that led me to send my last child to a childminder. With a childminder, there are several parents who can share experiences and who come and go at various times of day. In brief there is often more scrutiny of childminders than of sitters.

Childminding

At a common-sense level, the advantages of childminding appear to be that the child will have a close relationship with one adult, a 'family-like' atmosphere in a real home, and the company of a few familiar children. It sounds in many ways an ideal form of care, especially for the youngest children. Yet in the late 1960s and 1970s childminding got a very bad 'press'. The first studies of childminding in inner city areas told a bleak and often horrific story of neglected, depressed children kept in crowded and unstimulating conditions. It was believed that there were hundreds of thousands of children kept in the care of unregistered childminders (those who were not subject to the requirements of the social services departments), and that the care in these cases was appalling. Now, in contrast, the DHSS recommends childminding as the solution to the problems of working mothers – one that of course costs the government almost nothing. Why these differences? Has the quality of childminding changed? What is the picture of childminding today that we get from the recent studies that have been carried out?

There has certainly been a great deal of activity in the last ten years by local authorities to support childminders: to develop toy libraries that they can use, to loan equipment, to increase contacts between childminders and playgroups, to set up discussion groups between minders, and so on. And an important and energetic organization, the National Childminding Association, has grown up to campaign for better conditions and a change in the recognition of childminders. From the National Childminding Association, a minder can get information and support, advice and encouragement about how to make childminding satisfying for her, and stimulating and enjoyable for the children in her care. By 1984 10,000 women belonged to the NCMA, and the numbers are growing.

Is the life of a child at the minder's then quite different from the bleak picture painted by the researchers in the 1960s and 1970s? From recent studies we have the beginnings of some answers to the question, though there is still a great deal that we do not know about the consequences for different children of being at a childminder (see Bruner, 1980; Bryant, Harris and Newton, 1980; Mayall and Petrie, 1983; NCMA Topical Information Paper No. 1, 1984). First, who becomes a minder?

Most childminders are mothers of young or school-aged children who take on the job not for the money (which is pitifully small) but because they enjoy being with children, do not wish to go out to work, and want company for their own children. They are unlikely to have been trained in any way for child care. Most tend to see their role as 'caring for' the children, not educating or stimulating them. Second, what is life at the minder's like? For some children with some minders, it can be an extremely happy and successful arrangement; however, studies of childminding have shown us that for others it doesn't work out so well, and there are some points from this research worth noting if you are considering looking for a childminder. For many children, being at a minder's is unlikely to be a psychological 'home-from-home'. While most childminders are affectionate and concerned for their charges, in many cases the relationship between child and minder is not that of a substitute mother and her child, but something more detached. The studies of childminding stress that it is misleading to suggest that childminding is *homelike* in this sense. However they do show that at least outside the inner-city areas children are not in overcrowded or inadequate situations, they often have plenty of toys and playspace, varied routines with outings, and that many minders do play with their charges for at least some of the day. And the research has revealed some advantages to the minded child that are not often stessed. Minded children often develop close attachments and friendships with the other children at the minder's, and indeed with the minder's husband or parents. These 'extended family' relationships may be particularly rewarding to the single child of a single parent.

The researchers who've studied childminding do voice concerns, however: they stress that a worrying number of minded children appear withdrawn, quiet or sad. But we don't know that this is a *consequence* of being minded. The children who seem rather depressed at the minders are most often those who have suffered problems at home. What lessons from this research are useful for mothers who are about to make arrangements for childminding?

First, it is worth 'shopping around' before making a choice about a minder, rather than settling on the first minder with a vacancy. In the initial conversation, try to get at more than just an impression of the minder's friendliness to you. Talk to her and judge for yourself whether her experiences with children have taught her lessons that you wish to have inflicted on your child. Some parents want a warm, grandmotherly person to indulge their baby; others want a no-nonsense stimulating teacher. Talk to her to find out about the kind of day your child would spend with her. How much TV do the children watch? How much of the day would your child spend going from the minder's to the shops, or to school to pick up older children? Outings are fine but you don't want your child to spend most of the day on the road. How many children are in full-time care and how many, if any, come for after-school care? Some pleasant morning homes turn into bedlam when two four-year-olds and three primary school children join the two little ones in the living room after school. And while you talk to her, watch the children who are already being minded. Are they simply sitting, or playing in a concentrated way? Do they approach the minder and sit on her knee? Later in the chapter we spell out in more detail some of the ways in which a parent can judge the care that a child is likely to receive in a particular setting.

Second, once you have arranged with a childminder for your child to go regularly, it is best to introduce your child gently: give him a chance to get to know her, and to settle in slowly. Children who are picked up from a new nursery school by a strange minder and taken to her house may well have a hard time. If it is at all possible for the minder to visit you and your child at *your* home, it can be a great help: the minder can get an idea of how your child behaves in his own home, and she'll be better placed to judge how happy he is when he is with her. She may also find it easier to talk with you about any problems in his behaviour that may crop up. And that is important. Many parents and minders don't find it easy to talk about problems they may be having with the child – they each feel too defensive. Yet communication between mother and childminder about unhappy behaviour or aggression is vital if the child is to be helped over any problems.

Childminders who belong to a supportive network of minders, such as the groups affiliated to the National Childminding Association, are likely to provide better environments for the children in their care than those who have no contact with other minders or support systems. The minder who belongs to a network is not a lonely mother isolated out there in the community, but someone who will get advice and encouragement about the job of caring for children.

In sum, spending the day with a warm, affectionate and interested childminder can be a successful form of care for babies and toddlers, provided contact and communication between mother and minder about the baby's well-being is good, and that both are sensitive to any problems the child may experience – provided, too, that there is continuity of care, and that the child does not have to cope with a succession of different childminders. However, most pre-school children can enjoy and take advantage of the stimulation that a playgroup or nursery school can provide, and if your three-to four-year-old is with a minder, it is well worth trying to arrange for him to spend part of the day at a playgroup or nursery school. Very few of these can cater for the needs of the children of full-time working parents – they simply are not open for long enough hours. However for a very few mothers there may also be the possibility of a place at a nursery. The numbers of such available places is tiny; within local authority nurseries, priority is given to children considered to be at risk. But since the range of differences between nurseries is huge, it is worth a brief look at how these differences are likely to affect your child, and at how you can best assess the quality of a nursery if you are lucky enough to have one with vacancies nearby.

Day Nurseries

Day nurseries are staffed centres where children can be left for the whole day in the company of a group of children. A good day nursery includes the same kinds of materials and opportunities that a good nursery school offers. Part of each day is devoted to nursery-school activities such as singing, cutting and paperwork, talking with teachers, counting, painting and drawing, pretending, playing house, and all the myriad things that three- and four-year-olds love to do, especially in the company of other children. Few homes, yours or anyone else's, can offer as rich a variety of materials and activities with interested and trained caregivers *and* lots of companions, as a good nursery school.

Day nurseries are more institutional than childminders or your own home with a babysitter. Institutions are not necessarily bad, if they offer more extensive opportunities for playing, structured educational experiences, and more expert caregivers. All these qualities are recommended for most older pre-school children. Babies and toddlers may get along perfectly well in nurseries that specialize in making a home-like atmosphere – something that the kibbutzim in Israel have developed with great success. Some day-care centres in the US have family groups of four babies per caregiver and small private rooms for each group. The fact that there are 100 babies and children in the centre as a whole is irrelevant to each baby's experience, if she is cared for entirely in a small family group. What *is* relevant to your baby's experience, as with childminding, is the continuity of caregivers. The best nurseries try to organize the staffing so that the children experience as little turnover in caregivers as possible.

One real problem in day nurseries is contagion. Colds, flu and contagious diseases spread like proverbial wildfire in large nurseries. There are always children with chicken pox and viral infections, so the parent of a child at day nursery can count on her child being exposed to every disease in town. However babies do need to acquire immunity to various contagious diseases; most of the serious ones, such as measles, mumps and polio are now controlled by immunization that your baby will have before, or soon after, starting with a minder or at a nursery. The less serious contagious diseases, such as colds and flu, just have to be tolerated at this point. Your baby is more likely to encounter the minor contagions in earlier years of his life if he's at a day nursery than if he is with a minder or at home with a babysitter.

Day nurseries are under the supervision of the social services department of your area. Local authority nurseries must meet regulations on hygiene, safety, staffing and so on; fees in 1984 averaged £25 per week, but parents may qualify for a means-tested subsidy. Private nurseries may be financed and organized in a wide variety of ways – indeed the philosophy and organization of nurseries, both local authority and private, vary greatly. We don't have much research yet in Britain that allows us to judge very precisely what the different effects of these different nurseries may be on the children who go to them, but there are some features of the nurseries' organization and atmosphere that are important for parents to note. For instance, one study of day nurseries in London showed that, as Jerome Bruner noted,

> there are certain fundamental decisions that go into the organization of a nursery – fairly few in number, but highly pervasive in their effect – that express themselves from the start in the kind of nursery environment that they produce and the functions they permit a nursery to fulfil (Bruner, 1980, p. 142).

The 'house style' varies from very permissive to very strict. The priorities of the staff may be for tidiness and obedience, for an educational curriculum that must be gone through, or for 'open' child-directed activities.

The extent of structure or routine can vary greatly. The 'open' classroom can offer a rich variety of activities, if it is well run by competent nurses or teachers who support whatever the children might like to do with their time. If it is poorly run it can be chaos, in which arguments over materials and aimlessness prevail. At worst, an open classroom can look like *Lord of the Flies*, where the bullies subjugate and terrorize the less aggressive children. In a well-run open class, the children are free to choose how they spend their time and to pursue their own 'thing' for more concentrated periods than in more structured programmes.

Highly structured programmes aim to direct children's attention to a planned sequence of activities, which are thought to be developmentally appropriate for the average child of the age group. Well-run structured nurseries keep the children busy at useful and entertaining activities and help them to develop new capabilities by making sure that they are introduced to various and novel pursuits. A child who is afraid to get dirty may actually learn to enjoy finger painting; one who can't be bothered to get clean may actually learn how to wash her hands thoroughly. On the other hand, poorly run structured nurseries can be like prison camps, where the inmates are marched through set routines without regard to their individual interests or wishes. A child who hates big blocks may be pushed into building a castle when he would much prefer to be looking at books.

Most striking – and probably most important of all from the children's point of view – are the differences between nurseries in the kinds of relationships that the adults in the nurseries have with the children. Where adults in a nursery are very marked in their directiveness, this affects both the way in which the children play, and the kinds of conversation that they have. These turn into exchanges which are essentially teacher-tells-child, child-assents. And the differences between nurseries are marked in the extent to which the style of exchange between adults and children is 'cooperative' rather than 'confrontational' over issues of control, discipline and order, as well as in the extent to which formal education is emphasized. The primary contrast underlying these differences, argue Caroline Garland and Stephanie White, who have studied these nurseries, is between two assumptions about the nature of children, and the goals of the nursery that follow from these assumptions – note the parallel with our Watsonian and Gesellian children:

> When the *underlying assumption* is that the child is a thinking, feeling individual with needs, attitudes and opinions of its own, the nursery's *predominant goal* is likely to be enabling the development of satisfying social and emotional relationships. In *practice*, this will be manifested in a number of ways, of which the most obvious are a democratic style of management for the staff, and a day in which the larger part will be spent in 'free play': that is, in an activity and with the companions of the child's choice. The predominant style of control will be *cooperative* and the 'permitting' rather than the 'restricting' style of adult will be apparent . . .
>
> In contrast is the kind of nursery that maintains a *negative alliance*. Here the *underlying assumption* that the child is a primitive chaotic creature until controlled and shaped by the adults' superior strength and wisdom is associated with a *predominant goal* of promoting cognitive growth and the acquisition of skills. This will be manifested *in practice* by a hierarchic staff management system, and a day in which the child spends most of its time in a group whose size, composition and goal are determined by the adults. A *confronting* style of control will predominate, and adults will tend to be restricting rather than permitting in function. (Garland and White, 1980, p. 114).

The conclusions of this particular group of researchers are that the first set of assumptions and goals best suit children who are to spend all day in a nursery.

> A commitment to the child as he is, seeking his own expression and pursuing his own goals – rather than a judgemental approach in terms of adult norms – is the best assurance of the child's basic security in the nursery. (Bruner, 1980, p. 167).

On common-sense grounds it seems that some structure and some openness is usually the best compromise in a day nursery. A day that includes times when the child can pursue whatever interests her and other times when she is introduced to new and potentially exciting interests strikes a balance between the two extremes. As Sally Provence advised in Chapter 7, children need to learn both self-direction and compliance to the wishes of others. Life requires both. But the attitude of the staff to the children and to each other is of major importance in determining how the daily routine in practice will affect the children.

Playgroups, nursery schools and nursery classes

Let's look briefly at the three types of part-time provision available for children over three – playgroups, nursery schools and classes. These clearly do not provide care for the children of full-time working mothers, or for babies and toddlers. However they are, according to the 1980 OPCS national survey, used by 8 per cent of full-time and 7 per cent of part-time working mothers (Martin and Roberts, 1984). (A recent survey by the Pre-School Playgroups Association of 459 mothers in thirty-two playgroups reports that 28 per cent of the mothers in the playgroups had paid employment, usually part-time but varying greatly in extent. However, they did not all work during the hours that their children were at the playgroup (Research and Information Committee, PPA, 1982).) It is often possible to arrange for children who are looked after by a babysitter or childminder to be taken to a playgroup or nursery school or class. What kind of experiences are they likely to have there, and what differences are there between the three forms of provision?

Playgroups are voluntary groups in which a minimum of six children are looked after by some of the mothers of the children who attend. The sessions are usually two or three hours long. Most playgroups are affiliated with the Pre-School Playgroups Association, which encourages mothers to take part in the operation of the group, and organizes training courses for its group leaders. The general philosophy of the PPA is *not* towards 'educating' the children, rather the aim is to provide them with the opportunity of playing with each other, and to encourage mothers to enjoy and participate in their children's world of play. The role of the PPA is not directive: playgroups are highly autonomous, local groups, that organize themselves. They differ widely in focus, in the degree of structure, in the fees charged, and in the extent of parent participation.

Nursery schools in Britain are state schools, part of a long tradition of nursery education, frequently very concerned with the development of creativity and expressiveness in individual children. The teachers are highly trained – though among the lowest paid in the educational system. Nursery classes are also part of the state educational system: free of charge, they are administratively part of the primary schools. The teachers in nursery classes, unlike those in nursery schools, are usually trained in the teaching of primary school children.

Do the experiences of children differ greatly in these three forms of part-time provision? It is a question investigated recently as part of the Oxford Pre-school Project – a series of studies which looked in detail at the quality of children's play, concentration, conversation and interaction with adults in playgroups, nursery schools and classes of differing size and organization. The results showed that

> structure, intimacy and staffing ratio (the number of staff to children) seem, in the main, to matter more than whether the place is called a playgroup, a nursery class or a nursery school (Bruner, 1980, p. 73).

The quality of the children's play was most mature when the children played in *pairs* rather than alone or in larger groups; when the group as a whole was small – 70 per cent of the play of the older children in the smaller centres was 'elaborated', as compared to only a half in the larger ones; when the adults provided a stabilizing approving presence, and introduced the children to challenging tasks. And both among the older and younger children, more 'elaborated' play was generated in the more structured settings, not only when the children were engaged in the prescribed activities but during free play (see Sylva, Roy and Painter, 1980).

The range of activities and experiences possible for a three- to four-year-old in the best playgroups, nursery schools or classes are unlikely to be found at home with a babysitter or minder. It is clearly worth trying to arrange for your child to enjoy such experiences. If you are able to visit different playgroups or nurseries you can check how they compare on the 'criteria' that we list next, for those who may be about to make arrangements for their children's care.

Evaluating the Quality of Care

At the moment the only way to be assured of high quality care for your baby is to judge it for yourself. And the only way to judge it is to watch what goes on – whether you are considering childminding or a babysitter, or have the chance of a nursery place. The trouble is that many are not sure exactly what to look for. If the caregiver is friendly to the parents, does that indicate that she will take good care of the child, and be affectionate and warm? Let us examine some criteria for the best child care.

There are no statutory government standards of good child care, but there are guidelines that are generally agreed upon in the child development community. Alison Clarke-Stewart (1982), an authority on day care in the United States, says that observation of the actual situation is your best guarantee of quality. Nothing can replace the eyes and mind of the informed parent.

Use your knowledge of your own child, of what is appropriate for his age and stage, his personality and experience, to evaluate the care. No one can assess the care that is best suited to your own child better than you can. But here are some guidelines for selecting care that's appropriate for the average baby and pre-school child. The guidelines are drawn from the *Early Childhood Environment Rating Scale* (Harms and Clifford, 1980), from Alison Clarke-Stewart's *Daycare* (1982) and from our own research on child-care settings (SS). Most of what we describe can be observed in a half-hour visit. Other issues can be determined by talking to the caregivers. Others are things to be aware of after your child has started with the caregiver, when you are leaving him with her, and when you are picking him up. The keys to good care are, as always, that it is affectionate, sensitive to individual differences, and appropriate for the child's age and stage.

Happy children: do the babies and children appear happy and involved in play? Perhaps the most important litmus test for any child-care setting is how the children appear to you as you watch. Children in good care will look happy and involved, whereas those in poor care will be wandering aimlessly, crying, fighting with each other to a much greater extent. They look bored, and they are. Depressed children, withdrawn children, children who appear to be in a trance – these are signs of poor caretaking. Don't be seduced by an 'open classroom' excuse, if you're watching in a nursery. A true open classroom is a well-organized environment where children can happily choose their own activities; it is not a disorganized, impoverished setting.

Physical care: do the children get timely and pleasant meals and snacks? For babies under two, this means that the adults hold babies to give them their bottles when the child is hungry, feed regular meals to those on solid foods, and talk to the babies as they feed them. For pre-school children, good nutrition, regular meals and snacks, and friendly adult conversation are essential. Children's food preferences should be respected even if they are also encouraged to try new dishes. Some places have a haphazard schedule, non-nutritious foods, little adult interaction, a stifling atmosphere, or all of the above. Ask yourself: if you were a baby or a three- to four-year old, would you enjoy eating at this place?

Do the children get adequate rest and naps? The space for napping should be generous, quiet, well ventilated and supervised. Children should be helped to get to sleep by having their favourite toys or blankets. Respect should be shown for children who need more or less sleep in the afternoon, by allowing for early or late risers. Poor sleep arrangements include crowded, stuffy, noisy rooms, rigidly scheduled naptimes, and no attention to individual differences in napping.

Are the children reasonably clean? It's all very nice to finger paint, build sandcastles and crawl around the floor, but there comes a time to be cleaned up before eating or going home. Children who spend a whole day with the minder or in the nursery should be encouraged to wash their hands and even faces, brush their teeth after meals, and generally practise sanitary routines at some times during the day. Older children should be given experience with independence in these routines. Depending on your preference you may care more or less about cleanliness, but at least babies' nappies ought to be changed as needed. Neglect of hygiene or haphazard routines can be dangerous to your child's health. In our opinion, so can over-zealous concerns with neatness and cleanliness.

Play materials: are there enough books, toys, games and opportunities for varied play? The materials for babies and pre-school children should include those for quiet independent play, such as books, puzzles and bricks of various sizes; those for more social play, such as costumes, household objects, dolls, stuffed animals and puppets; and those for making things and pictures, such as clay, paints and crayons. Children should have access to safe play materials and be provided with good supervision for the use of saws, hammers, knives and so on. Babies should have varied experiences with shapes, soft and hard toys, containers – and all the objects that they play with should be safe.

Does the space available to the children allow for both harmonious play with the other children, and individual choices of how to spend time? Crowded spaces do not allow for much variety of activities. Rooms for babies should have rugs to sit and crawl on; what's needed are places where children can look at books, do puzzles, play house and build; and outdoor spaces for riding tricycles, swinging, climbing, hiding, running and jumping. Crowded and monotonous spaces do not make for good child care.

Is the place attractively decorated and arranged from the child's point of view? In a nursery can children see pictures? If the rooms are meant for the children's benefit, they will have low, open shelves for safe toys, closed cupboards up high for materials the caregivers need to keep under control, and bright attractive wall decorations where children can see them. A childminder's house obviously cannot be judged by the same exclusively child-oriented criteria as a day nursery, but it is reasonable to expect it to be attractive, comfortable, safe and clean. If the walls are peeling, the cupboards are all closed, many toys are broken, or the room is a wreck from the previous day, ask yourself if this is what you want for your child.

Do the minder or the nursery staff know enough about children to provide good care? Some training in child development or education is your best guarantee that the caregivers know what to expect of babies and young children, and that they will respect individual differences among children. Mothers of more than one child are also, in our experience, more likely to understand how young children develop and how different they can be from one another. Talk with the minder or the day-nursery staff about their experience with babies and young children, and their training, before you entrust your child to their care.

Are the babies and children supervised closely but not intrusively? If there is safe space and safe materials, the adults can supervise without intruding on the children's solitary or social play, unless the latter becomes too antagonistic. Disputes can be important learning occasions for young children, if the grown-up can help them to learn to negotiate the use of wanted materials (taking turns), settle priority issues (me first), and overcome problems of participation ('me too'). It is not helpful if the person in charge orders settlements along adult lines, because children do not always think like adults and do not always understand the principles of an adult-imposed treaty. They need to negotiate child-style but to be protected from abuses of one another.

Is there careful supervision of the babies in potentially dangerous spaces, and the children with potentially dangerous material? Needless to say, you want your child to be safe. Babies need protection from falling down stairs and from falling off adult-sized furniture. Three- and four-year-olds need protection from sharp and pointed objects and from other children who are physically aggressive. It can be quite appropriate for children to have opportunities to experiment with hammering, or with cutting celery, but adults must be close at hand to prevent injury. Babies need experience of pulling themselves up to stand against furniture and climbing stairs, but they need adults to catch them on the way down.

Is every opportunity to talk with the babies and children used? Children learn most about the world through communication with adults. Both experiences with the physical world, and exchanges with other people, need interpretation – names for things, feelings, relations and needs, explanations for why things happen, and for why people behave the way that they do. Conversations and discussions all through the day, whether reading stories, talking about the feel of sand, or describing how to sweep with a broom – that is what to look for. Are the babies' pointing gestures responded to? Are the children's questions answered? Adults should listen to what children say and ask, and respond appropriately. Cooperative conversations, talking and listening, are good indices of a good setting.

Daily routine: are there regular times of the day for reading, music, painting and outdoor play, for free play and play alone? As we've noted, a good day for the children is semi-structured in that there are some regularly scheduled activities, and plenty of space for the children's individual preferences.

Are there times when the children are alone and times when they are doing things together with other children? For babies and toddlers, being together in a group has limited value. It's more important that they are getting lots of individual attention from adults. For older pre-school children, being in a group with other children and an adult requires social skills that need to be learnt – in small doses. They need to learn to listen to a teacher when she talks to ten children at once; to sit still and listen to a story; to hear a visitor talking about guitar strings; to wait in a queue at the library. These are important social skills for three- and four-year-olds. Small groups are easier to handle, both for the children and for the adults. A group of two or three pre-school-aged children for an activity is less demanding and less frustrating to themselves and to adults than larger groups, because each child gets a greater chance to participate and to express himself. Most of the child's day should be spent with a *few* others, doing what *he* chooses to do.

Relations with parents: in a nursery, how do the staff communicate with the parents about their children's activities, development, problems and special talents? There should be plenty of opportunity for meetings between parents and the staff, both with parents as a group and with individual parents. Parents need to know about the nursery as a whole and about their own child's progress and happiness within it. Staff in a nursery may have a helpful perspective on individual children, because they have experience with many children; most parents know only their own children and those of a few friends. Depending on their training and experience, the perspective of the nursery staff may be more or less informed; regardless of their competence, you at least need to know how they view your child. Ask them if there are regular meetings between parents and staff.

Is the child's transition from home to minder or nursery and back again eased by those in charge? On arriving in the morning, children should be greeted enthusiastically, even if they are not eager to be left by their parents. Similarly, in the afternoons, the child should be bid goodbye with warmth and anticipation of the next day, whether or not she is warm in return. Parents should be helped to ease their child over the transition and separation by a minder or caregiver who is confident that all will work out well in the long run. And parents should be helped to ease their child back to the family world even if the child seems to prefer being at the minder's or nursery twenty-four hours a day. The key is communication between parents, minders and children about the expectations for each one. Talk and ask.

These questions can be useful guides on what to look for, when you're with a potential childminder or in a nursery. We suggest that you use them to help you decide what you want for your own child, and to decide what will suit your child best. Some children enjoy and need more outdoor physical activity, while others wish that they never had to put a coat on to leave the house. Some thrive in the company of other children, while others prefer the company of an adult.

If you manage to visit a number of minders or nurseries you will find, as we did in our research, that good things in child care go together (McCartney *et al.*, 1982; McCartney *et al.*, 1983). Good care is good and bad is bad in so many ways. Childminders or nurseries in which the relationships between children and adults are warm and cooperative and there are lots of play materials, usually also provide nutritious meals, some organized activities, and have patterns of feeding and napping that take account of the individual needs of different children. Poor care situations have overworked adults, few play materials, less nutritious meals and children who are bored or sad, or create chaos. If you see in the midmorning that the toddlers at a minder's are wandering about doing nothing and the babies are stashed away in their cots, you can be fairly sure that this place is not going to provide the care you want your child to have. If, on the other hand, the children seem to be happily involved, the minder or day-nursery nurse talks to each child in the course of a half-hour or so, and there are bountiful toys, you do not have to stay for lunch to find out if the food is good. A balanced meal is very likely to be served, that your child won't eat.

Let's assume that you are planning a visit to a minder or a nursery. Good times to visit are in the morning or in the late afternoon, when the children are up from their naps. The first hours in the morning can be very revealing. How are greetings and goodbyes handled, especially for those children who are distressed when Daddy leaves? Is there an enthusiastic welcome for the children? Are there interesting things to do, ready for the child to start the day? How are distressed babies comforted?

At any time in the morning or mid to late afternoon you should be able to see how the needs of the children are managed, both as individuals and as a group. You can compare what you see with the list of questions we have outlined. For instance, is there time for the babies to be cuddled and played with? Is each child individually talked to and smiled at? For the toddlers and older children, is there a chance to paint or to play outside? What happens if it is raining?

In a day nursery, do talk to the head about her philosophy of child care. Ask her about what she considers priorities. What does she believe is most important in the care of babies and young children? If she does not understand what you are talking about, go elsewhere. A trained head understands that different nurseries emphasize one approach or another, depending on what the managers think are their major responsibilities to the children, and how they view the staff organization in the nursery. Does she emphasize orderliness and obedience, freedom and self-expression, or a mixture of the two? Does she see the pre-school years as carefree exploration or as intensely important learning experiences? Depending on your own views on child rearing, you may wish to find care that emphasizes control or permissiveness, self-expression or instruction – all of which can suit children perfectly if not carried to extremes.

Back-up Systems

No matter which kind of care you choose, something is bound to go wrong from time to time. Babysitters get ill, take holidays, have dying relatives, and don't come when there's a bus strike. Childminders also get ill, take holidays, have dying relatives, and you can't get to them when there's a bus strike. They are less likely than sitters to care for your child when he is ill, as he inevitably will be, because other children will be exposed. Day nurseries are even touchier about mildly ill children, because of contagion, but a nursery does not close when one caregiver is ill.

Nurseries usually have the least flexible hours; children may not arrive before X hour or depart after Y hour. What do you do if you have to work late, or the car breaks down? Working parents depend heavily on the tirelessness and good health of every one in the family, and there are bound to be times when the precarious system breaks down. The lucky parents are those who can have a flexible schedule themselves. Understanding employers, self-employment and part-time work all buffer the problems of a breakdown in the care arrangements. Another back-up is collaboration with other parents whose child-care arrangements can be shared with yours when needed. If your babysitter can look after their children at a pinch, theirs can look after yours in similar emergencies, especially if all parents agree that children's exposure to minor illnesses is a small price to pay for peace of mind. If you are willing to pick up their children from their minder on the days that they cannot make it, they will be willing to help you out in the same way.

Friends who are full-time mothers will often play substitute caregiver in a real emergency, although they may be disapproving about your working in the first place. Understandably, they are not eager to relieve working parents of their guilt, or shore up their shaky arrangements. Sometimes there is a neighbour who does not want regular responsibility for children but who is willing to help out when you really need her.

A few of us can actually take our children to work, if necessary. Our own children have attended lectures, sat in on meetings and eaten lunch at college or faculty clubs when child-care arrangements crashed. Armed with colouring books, favourite blankets and toys, they have all gone to work with one or the other parent when all else failed. Not many parents have this privilege, but it works well. Children enjoy the special treat, and parents get through yet another child-care crisis.

The real problem in all child-care arrangements is that they are individually gerrymandered solutions to a common parental problem – how to provide high quality care while parents work. There ought to be community child-care arrangements with built-in back-up systems, so that parents can work without anxiety about their children's welfare, and are not forced to work anti-social hours, or to fit all their other responsibilities around a precarious set of child-care arrangements. Each of us has to face crises in our arrangements for our children: the crises are met and coped with, somehow – but they are yet another drain on a mother's energy and resources. It is not how it should be – for mothers or for their children.

CHAPTER TEN

Child Care: Everybody's Business

We think of child care as a private family concern, a matter for mothers and fathers, not for government pronouncements. Yet what happens to our young children *is*, already, profoundly affected by policies, or the lack of them. This is the case not just for families in extreme need, or under great stress, vulnerable to policies on welfare and social support. The quality of all our children's daily lives, and the pattern of their futures, are affected, directly and indirectly, purposely and inadvertently, by decisions on health services, social services, taxation, employment for women, rates, housing policies, and so on. It may be an accumulation of small unrelated decisions – often decisions to do nothing, in Sir Humphrey's accomplished 'Yes Minister' style – but it adds up to an involvement of the state in children's lives that must be acknowledged. It may be a *laissez-faire* line that's favoured, but it is still in effect a policy. The decision to do nothing is still a decision.

Moreover, the care of young children is and should be a matter of public interest and responsibility, as well as a matter of private joy and responsibility. This is not a matter of dispute as far as children's *health* is concerned; why should their emotional and educational needs be less important?

To recognize public responsibility for the quality of children's lives and the lives of their mothers becomes all the more urgent when we admit what the quality of those lives is like for so many people in Britain today. We *know* that the social and economic changes in Britain have profoundly affected family life. The details do not have to be spelt out; they are all too clear to anyone who cares to look beyond the homes of the affluent. Four instances will suffice. First, unemployment has a shattering impact on family life (Sinfield, 1978). As Jerome Bruner points out, 'Not to respond to that fact once it is known is in effect to take a stand on policy'

(Bruner, 1980, p. 2). Second, over a quarter of mothers with young children are on tranquillizers for depressive illnesses. That spells trouble for children. Third, single parents – dramatically increasing in numbers – are very likely to be below the poverty line, and thus under both economic and emotional stress. Again, children's welfare is threatened. And fourth, a theme of this book, the numbers of women with young children who work is steadily increasing, while the provision for the care and education of those children is steadily decreasing.

These are features of life in Britain today that are well documented and are accepted to be the case; they are not new problems but they are growing in scale. Each affects the quality of children's lives. Provision of good child care outside the family would diminish each of them. To have no coherent policy on child care outside the family in the face of these needs is a staggering failure in a nation whose record on social and welfare policies has historically often been one of imagination and courage.

But the case for child-care provision outside the home should not be made solely on the grounds of the urgent social needs of the most vulnerable families in our society. Those desperate needs highlight the urgency of the case, but it is a case that should be made on two quite other separate grounds, grounds that apply to all mothers and all children in Britain.

Inequality

The first concerns women as mothers and as employed people. Women are markedly disadvantaged, in comparison with men, in employment, in the professions, in politics, in trade unions, and in public life generally. The reasons for this inequality are many, complicated and inter-linked. One reason, however, stands out: it is the hugely differential effect of parenthood on women and on men – the disproportionate share of responsibility that falls on women. Once women have children, and leave their employment in order to care for those dependent children, they are unlikely to be able to return to employment at the same level: the OPCS National Survey in 1980 showed that 45 per cent of women going back to a part-time job after childbearing experience downward occupational mobility. The more a woman delays her first return to work after childbearing, the more likely she is to return to a lower-level occupation. It is part-time working that is particularly associated with downward mobility: women who first return to work full time after a child's birth, then change to part time work, are particularly likely to experience downward mobility (Martin and Roberts, 1984). On average, a woman takes seven years out of the labour market for each child, and over a lifetime she earns half the wages of a man (Joshi, 1984; 1985).

The importance of these figures is that they show just how misleading is the following argument, so often put forward as a reason against mothers' working: 'Surely women can take a few years off from their employment while their children are young, and need them – then they can return to work and their other activities after the children have grown up. Isn't the care and comfort of children more important than a few years' employment?'

If the care and comfort of children *were* to be jeopardized by a mother's employment, very few mothers would choose to take that risk. But it is clear now from decades of research, and from the experience of other countries, that children's welfare is not threatened or jeopardized by their mother's working *per se*. There need be no conflict of interests between those of the child and those of the mother, if the care available is good. What threatens children's welfare and happiness is the experience of growing up in stressful, discordant and unhappy homes, or in poor child-care environments, not the experience of having a mother who works.

To make the sharing of child-care responsibility more equitable between women and men is one of the policy goals that is most heavily stressed by the National Childcare Campaign. As a recent discussion paper published by the NCC makes clear:

> A primary objective of policy therefore should be the equitable sharing of the demands and responsibilities that arise from the care of dependent children. A second and related objective should be to enable parents to combine parenthood with employment and other valued and enhancing public activities with a minimum of difficulty and tension . . . The overall aim should be that parenthood does not leave women at a disadvantage in

employment, politics or other areas of public life, and does not impose excessive demands on them that currently produce so much stress and unhappiness. If this sounds rather ambitious, to place our expectations into perspective, we aim to provide women with the same deal from parenthood that most men get from it at present (NCC, 1985, p. 4).

Provision for pre-school children should not be seen as the 'shoring up' of the families of a number of women who have failed as individuals to cope adequately with their children and lives. It should be seen as one way to redress the inequalities and stresses that the structure of our society places on women with children. It is not an individual problem, but a problem of our society.

Cost or Benefit to Children?

A second set of grounds for the case for child-care provision concerns the possible *benefit* to our children. One of our most distinguished developmental psychologists, Jerome Bruner, summed up the results of research into nursery schools, playgroups, childminders and day nurseries that he headed in Oxford as follows:

> The full-time care of children at home in the family in the years preceding school is neither desirable for many families nor, given that fact, is it good for children. Indeed, it can now be taken as certain that an opportunity to be away from home in a pre-school helps the child develop socially, intellectually and emotionally (Bruner, 1980, p. 198).

The case for pre-school provision for children then rests not just on the demonstration that it need not be a disadvantage for them to be away from their mothers, even as babies under two years old, but on the positive benefits and the undoubted pleasures that it can give them.

Policy Issues

To underline the public, communal responsibility for child care is not to advocate 'state intervention' in the way that parents choose to look after their children. It is not in any way to diminish the responsibility or the choice that parents have for the way that their children spend their early years. Rather, it is to advocate an increase in that choice and in the abilities of parents to provide their children with the experiences they would like them to have. When parents were asked what they wanted to have available for their children, back in 1974, 90 per cent of parents of three- to four-year-olds and 46 per cent with under-threes wanted some form of nursery place (Office of Population and Censuses Survey). Other surveys since then report similar figures, and an increasing demand for full day care. In the recent OPCS survey of women and employment, 88 per cent of young women who had not yet had children said they intended to take no break from work when they had their children or to return to work before their children left school. In comparison with the survey in 1965, women in 1980 were more likely to stress their right to choose, and to stress employment rather than staying at home when they had strong views about what women should do (Martin and Roberts, 1984).

The demand for some kind of child care is unmistakable. Preferences for *what* kind differ – and should of course be respected. Mothers should be free to choose between a good childminder, a good nursery, nursery school or playgroup, or a sitter. The needs and wants of half the electorate and their children are clear. But politically, child care is nearly a dead issue because there is no clear constituency that supports a single policy and because children's issues are not money- or vote-getters (Beck, 1982, p. 312).

But although child-care issues are not high on any party or government platform, the problems and possibilities of provision for children under five have been examined by a number of groups, both government committees and energetic pressure groups such as the National Childcare Campaign. Back in 1978, the Central Policy Review Staff reported on *Services for Young Children with Working Mothers*, and stressed four outstanding problems with the existing services: the lack of priorities and direction as to ways in which the services should progress; the divided responsibility and fragmentation of administration of services; the inequitable consequences for children and parents of the present situation; the denial to a substantial number of children of the recognized benefits of education and care outside the home. The confusions and problems that were lucidly described by the CPRS report are still with us. For instance the divided responsibility for child-care provision – between educational and social services – that excludes the possibility of an overall policy on the under-fives still holds. This is in spite of government circulars such as the DES/DHSS Circular Letter of January 1978 that commented:

> No services for young children and their families can operate in isolation; almost everyone working in this field has much to gain from the expertise and experience of people in other statutory, voluntary and community services.

But nothing practically effective followed. The recommendations were for advisory committees responsible to both educational and social service committees – with *no* authority or executive powers.

Since the CPRS report we have had recommendations and policy proposals from a range of child-care experts, from the TUC, and from groups such as the National Childcare Campaign. The recommendations vary in the degree of caution, the radical nature of the revisions proposed, the funding suggested, and the priority given to social problems or to broader inequalities between women and men. The National Childcare Campaign has summarized the policy issues in a comprehensive, realistic and practical way. The group supports the development and integration of a variety of types of provision:

Free nursery education to all children whose parents wish it.

Local nursery centres or community nurseries which offer full day provision, combine care and education, employ and invite local people, and give them and the parents the chance to participate in the running of the centre.

Out of school care for nursery, primary and secondary school children.

Workplace nurseries.

Childminding which is properly supported, with training opportunities, resources and a guaranteed wage.

Flexible and integrated courses for child-care workers which cross the artificial boundaries between care and education.

The development of anti-racist strategies in all forms of provision and training.

The integration of children with special needs, with appropriate back-up resources.

Parental leave which gives either parent a generous right to time off for very young or sick dependants.

Adequate child benefit and family income support for those with young children.

The NCC encourages the diversity of types of service on the grounds that there are widely differing parental preferences that should be respected, and that it is important to encourage innovations in child-care provision. The recommendations also stress the coordination of voluntary and government agencies in providing care. In a discussion paper it is suggested that

> There is scope for a substantial input from non-statutory agencies, fully financially supported, though, by government funds.
>
> However, to be in receipt of public funds, non-statutory (and statutory) agencies should be expected to meet certain expectations. In particular each provision should:
>
> (i) offer a role in management to parents and workers . . .
>
> (ii) be publicly accountable for its values base, aims and performance.
>
> (iii) be subject to regular inspection to monitor quality.
>
> (iv) provide pay and conditions for all workers that conform with a uniform, integrated and national agreement covering all child-care workers (NCC, 1985, p. 10).

How such changes could be put into practical workable programmes has been thought about, discussed and set out in a number of publications by the NCC. It is clear that solutions to the administrative, legislative and financial problems involved in setting up, maintaining and monitoring child-care provision on the scale that's needed will not be quickly found. But they *can* be found, if the political will is there.

And at the level of organizing the care itself, we now know enough about what constitutes good care, and enough about the shortcomings of the present situation, to be practical. The studies of childminders, day nurseries, playgroups and nursery schools have given us clear messages on the strengths and weaknesses of each type of provision – messages on how to make each type of care more supportive, caring, interesting and challenging for the children. Meeting the shortcomings and inadequacies won't be easy or simple, of course; but if the energy and enthusiasm already evident in some of the innovative community schemes, extended play-groups, and collaborations between voluntary and statutory groups, is generously supported, they can and will be met. The lesson that such problems can be tackled and solved is there in our neighbouring countries, with their imaginative attempts to provide comprehensive and *good* care for children throughout the working day.

The example of Sweden is particularly telling. In the 1970s the expansion of child-care services was seen as the most important family policy issue. This was partly because of the conviction that child care could help to give children a good start in life, and partly as a response to the increase in numbers of working mothers with pre-school children. The programmes of child care are financed through a combination of rates, state subsidies stemming from employer payroll fees, and parents' fees. Provision is the responsibility of local authorities, regulated by the central government. Local authorities are required to plan ahead for demand. There is a diversity of types of care, including, for instance, childminding with an extensive support system. And the care is tuned-in to the real-life problems of parents: care for children who are ill is provided with peripatetic childminders – the employees of the local authorities – who care for the children in their own homes; out-of-school care for older children is run in the form of out-of-school clubs by the local authorities.

The issues of training are taken seriously. Childminders are required to take training, and are then employed by the local authorities; nursery nurses can take further training as nursery teachers. Curriculum planning for children of all ages – including the under-twos – is a matter for research. And policy concerning parental employment aims explicitly for full equality between men and women; either father or mother can take extended parental leave with job rights guaranteed (see *Childcare Programmes in Sweden*, Swedish Institute, 1984).

Britain's unwillingness to adopt the Scandinavian or Eastern European model of assuring good child care for everyone – because mothers are not to be encouraged to work – results in an odd dislocation in the policies towards children. We endorse public education for everyone, provided for by the government. To educate the future workers, taxes support children's daily supervision for most of a parent's working day. The right to child care and education at public expense begins at five and ends at eighteen. Why does the government suddenly become financially responsible for the daytime activities of children at five, and not at three or at one? Is there some theory about child development that espouses neglect in the first five years and care thereafter?

From those that have not . . .

At the time of writing, the government's policies are undermining even the pitifully small provision that we have. Local authorities used to receive 58 per cent of their budget from the government – the 'rate support grant'. This has now been cut to 51 per cent, which means that councils either have to cut services or increase rates. But the government has now set targets for each section of service in each council, and if the council spends more than the government target it has to pay a penalty, a sum deducted from the rate support grant. So, if a council decides to spend beyond the target specified by the government, the government will give it less. There is now legislation to forbid councils to raise the rates in order to provide services.

The councils in some of the poorest inner-city areas argue that they *have* to spend more, to deal with the massive problems of poverty, poor housing and unemployment – indeed it is the same councils who are receiving the most urban aid funds that are referred to as 'profligate' spenders by the government, and from whom the government demands the largest cuts. The cuts are apparently felt in all types of provision, both state and 'voluntary'. In nursery education, for instance, the effects are particularly striking, given Mrs Thatcher's support for nursery education in the 1970s. The nursery school figures (where no issue of maternal-employment-damaging-children arises) show a drop of 10,000 places between 1982–4. The figures the government usually presents include rising fives who are in infant schools: the actual percentage of three- to four-year-olds receiving nursery school education is only 22 per cent. The PPA stresses how cruelly local authority cuts will affect their work in the poorest parts of Britain:

> Without support from local authorities, most local branches and County Associations of PPA would find it impossible to continue their work at its current high standard. This is especially true in areas of high unemployment and low incomes where there is no hope of continual fundraising as a source of income (The Information Officer, PPA).

And the National Childminding Association also underlines how the quality of their 'private' care for children will be affected by cuts in local authority budgets. They emphasize that childminding is often seen as 'private' child care, but in fact, childminders are also dependent on local authority funding: for registration and support workers, for equipment and group facilities and for direct payments to help low-waged families.

Hope for the Future?

The response to the cutting of local authority support and services demonstrates one hopeful sign in this bleak picture – the increasing numbers of those actively involved in discussing and campaigning for pre-school provision: pressure groups such as the NCC, the Children's Legal Centre, the National Childminding Association, the National Council for One Parent Families. Another hopeful sign is the spread of local initiatives and innovatory schemes. Whenever and wherever funding for pre-school provision is available, groups wanting to develop and expand services appear. Most notable has been the response to the GLC's £3.5 million child-care programme. In the Borough of Southwark, alone, for instance, eighty different community groups, including church groups, tenants associations and adult education institutes, said that they wanted to develop or expand child-care services. It's a response that reflects both the demand for provision, and the resources of energy and imagination that people in all sectors are willing to devote to solving the problems of provision.

What about the policies of the other parties? The SDP pamphlet 'Education matters: Children First' makes clear that the SDP does not believe in a 'comprehensive state-run child care on demand'. Their concern is that a state service would devalue the cooperative, self-help nature of what in their view is the best provision – playgroups. Yet this is a non-starter as an argument. State funding could of course be used to fund flexible, locally based and controlled cooperative provision, as the Swedish model shows. The Labour Party 'Charter for the under-fives' highlights well the inadequacies and muddles in the present system, but gives no clear commitment to providing and funding child care.

Tax benefits? For others, not us

One way in which the financial costs of private child-care provision could be met is by tax benefits to the working parents. In a number of European countries such benefits enable working parents to pay for child care – France, The Netherlands, Greece, Luxemburg, for instance. In Canada, working parents receive an allowance of 1,250 dollars per annum per child for day care. In contrast, Britain provides no tax benefits for the costs of child care. In 1978 a divorced mother who worked as the single support for her two children fought for the right to deduct her expenses for babysitter and childminder as necessary for carrying out her job. She lost the case.

And the tax situation makes it likely that the few workplace nurseries that do at the moment operate in Britain will disappear. These nurseries are at present treated as taxable benefits-in-kind – a ludicrous situation which equates the crèche with a company yacht for the benefit of the managing director. There is no way that parents using crèches will be able to afford to pay the tax, and they do already pay substantial contributions to the cost out of their taxed earnings. Unless legislation is passed to remove the tax, Britain will be the only country in the EEC that collects tax from such nurseries. The irony is that a Conservative government should here be destroying the provision for those who are trying to help themselves rather than relying on the state – a second irony to follow the first, their undermining of the 'voluntary' PPA and private childminding care by slashing the support to local authorities.

Parents Determine Child Care

Children have no better advocates than their own parents. As a group, parents make up a majority of the country's voters. If child-care issues were truly advocated, we could have what we want and need. Our myths about parenthood and child care defeat our unity. Mothers should stay at home with their children, yes? Good fathers should provide single-handedly for the financial needs of their wives and children, yes? Families have the responsibility to provide care for their children, as long as they are under five, yes? These are myths that did not fit the nineteenth century well, and are grotesquely out of key now as we approach the twenty-first. Today's image of the perfect mother who is there at the kitchen table organizing her children's play, while cooking a gourmet meal and – somehow – also succeeding at professional life, is another myth, one that's guaranteed to fill anyone who attempts to live up to it with despair, unless she has great resources of financial, practical and emotional support.

And it's these myths that prevent parents from asserting their common interests to ensure good care for their children. Each of us believes that we should be able to cope independently. When we have difficulty juggling the impossibly demanding roles of these superhero mothers and fathers, we blame ourselves. The myths of the father-provider and mother-in-apron diffuse parents' combined interests in assuring good care for their children. Each of us is left alone, guilty of inadequacy, to work out some precarious solution to the problem that's common to all working parents: good care for our children while we work. The myths also exacerbate the desperate situation of so many families – single parents, those under economic stress – since they prolong the inaction of governments to provide for children outside the family.

In 1980 Bruner argued that it was the lack of public debate that lay behind the continuing muddle and confusion in our (lack of) services for young children. In a similar vein, Linda Challis argued that such debate about the future of services would have to wait until the consensus was organized into action/pressure groups and 'well-publicized instances of distress and injury caused by the lack of clarity about standards of day care' (Challis, 1980). Since then, there *are* more hopeful signs: the pressure groups of the National Childcare Campaign, the National Childminding Association working hard to improve the standards and status of childminding, the PPA striving to meet the demands of families other than the affluent, the hundreds of innovative schemes springing up to cope with the problems of urban working mothers, and groups battling to save nurseries from closing. It is on these initiatives, this energy and this enthusiasm that we must capitalize, together with our understanding of what pre-school children need and enjoy. And it is on care for children during their first five years that we must, together, *insist*.

References

Ainsworth, M. D. S. (1973) The development of infant-mother attachment. In Caldwell, B. M., and Ricciuti, H. N. (eds.) *Review of Child Development Research*, Vol. 3. New York: Academic Press.

Ainsworth, M. D. S., Blehar, M., Waters, E., and Wall, S. (1978) *Patterns of attachment: A Psychological Study of the Strange Situation*. Hillsdale, NJ: Erlbaum.

Bar-Tal, D., Raviv, A., and Shavit, N. (1981) Motives for helping behavior: Kibbutz and city children in kindergarten and school. *Developmental Psychology*, 17:766–72.

Beck, R. (1982) Beyond the stalemate in child care public policy. In Zigler, E. F., and Gordon, E. W. (eds.) *Day Care: Scientific and Social Policy Issues*, 307–37. Boston: Auburn House.

Beit-Hallahmi, B., and Rabin, A. I. (1977) The kibbutz as a social experiment and as a child-rearing laboratory. *American Psychologist*, 32:533–41.

Belsky, J., Lerner, R. M., and Spanier, G. B. (1984) *The Child in the Family*. Reading, Mass.: Addison-Wesley.

Belsky, J., and Steinberg, L. D. (1978) The effects of daycare: A critical review. *Child Development*, 49:929–49.

Berndt, T. J. (1981) Relations between social cognition, non-social cognition, and social behavior: The case of friendship. In Flavell, J. H., and Ross, L. (eds.) *Social Cognitive Development: Frontiers and Possible Futures*, 176–99. New York: Cambridge University Press.

Bettelheim, B. (1969) *The Children of the Dream*. New York: Macmillan.

Borstelmann, L. J. (1983) Children before psychology: Ideas about children from Antiquity to the late 1800s. In Mussen, P. (ed.) *Handbook of Child Psychology*, 1:1–40. New York: Wiley.

Bowlby, J. (1940a) Psychological Aspects. In Padley, R., and Cole, M. (eds.) *Evacuation Survey: A Report to the Fabian Society*, 186–96. London: Fabian Society.

Bowlby, J. (1940b) The influence of early environment in the development of neurosis and neurotic character. *International Journal of Psychoanalysis*, 21: 154–80.

Bowlby, J. (1969) Attachment. *Attachment and Loss*, Vol. 1. New York: Basic Books.

Bronfenbrenner, U., Alvarez, W. F., and Henderson, C. R., Jr (1983) *Working and watching: Maternal employment status and parents' perceptions of their three-year-old children*. Unpublished manuscript, Cornell University.

Bruner, J. (1980) *Under Five in Britain*. London: Grant McIntyre.

Bruner, J. (1983) *Child's Talk: Learning to Use Language*. New York: Norton.

Bryant, B., Harris, M., and Newton, D. (1980) *Children and Minders*. London: Grant McIntyre.

Cairns, R. B. (1983) The emergence of developmental psychology. In Mussen, P. (ed.) *Handbook of Child Psychology*, 1:1–102. New York: Wiley.

Caldwell, B. M., Wright, C. M., Honig, A. S., and Tannenbaum, J. (1970) Infant care and attachment. *American Journal of Orthopsychiatry*, 40:397–412.

Caplan, G. (1954) Clinical observations on the emotional life of children in the communal settlements of Israel. In Senn, M.S.E. (ed.) *Problems of Infancy and Childhood*. New York: Josiah Macy Foundation.

Central Advisory Council for Education (England) (1967) *Children and Their Primary Schools* (Plowden Report). London: HMSO.

Central Policy Review Staff (1978) *Services for Young Children with Working Mothers*. London: HMSO.

Challis, L. (1980) *The Great Under-Fives Muddle*. University of Bath.

Clarke, A. M., and Clarke, A. D. B. (1976) *Early Experience: Myth and evidence*. London: Open Books.

Clarke-Stewart, A. (1982) *Daycare*. Cambridge, Mass.: Harvard University Press.

Cohen, L. B. (1979) Our developing knowledge of infant perception and cognition. *American Psychologist*, 34:894–9.

Committee on Local Authority and Allied Personal Social Services (1968) *Report of the Committee* (Seebohm Report). London: HMSO.

Cowan, R. S. (1983) *More Work for Mother: The Ironies of Household Technology from the Open Hearth to the Microwave*. New York: Basic Books.

Crosby, F. (1982) *Relative Deprivation and Working Women*. New York/Oxford: Oxford University Press.

Degler, C. N. (1980) *At Odds: Women and the Family in America from the Revolution to the Present*. New York/Oxford: Oxford University Press.

Department of Education and Science (1972) *Education: A Framework for Expansion*. London: HMSO.

Douglas, J. W. B., and Blomfield, J. M. (1948) *Maternity in Great Britain*. London: Oxford University Press.

Dunn, J. (1980) Feeding and sleeping. In Rutter, M. (ed.) *Scientific Foundations of Developmental Psychiatry*, 119–28. London: Heinemann Medical Books.

Dunn, J. (1983) Sibling relationships in early childhood. *Child Development*, 54, 787–811.

Dunn, J. (1984) *Sisters and Brothers*. London: Fontana.

Dunn, J., and Kendrick, C. (1982) *Siblings: Love, Envy, and Understanding*. Cambridge, Mass.: Harvard University Press.

Eckerman, C. O., and Whatley, J. L. (1977) Toys and social interaction between infant peers. *Child Development*, 48:1645–56.

Eckerman, C. O., Whatley, J. L., and Kutz, S. L. (1975) The growth of social play with peers during the second year of life. *Developmental Psychology*, 11:42–49.

Ehrenreich, B., and English, D. (1979) *For Her Own Good: 150 Years of the Experts' Advice to Women*. New York: Doubleday/Anchor Press.

Eiduson, B. T., Kornfein, M., Zimmerman, I. L., and Weisner, T. S. (1982) Comparative socialization practices in traditional and alternative families. In Lamb, M. (ed.) *Nontraditional Families: Parenting and Child Development*, 315–46. Hillsdale, NJ: Erlbaum.

English, O. S., and Foster, C. J. (1953) *Fathers are Parents Too*. London: George Allen and Unwin.

Erikson, E. H. (1950) *Childhood and Society*. New York: Norton.

Etaugh, C. (1980) Effects of nonmaternal care on children: Research evidence and popular views. *American Psychologist*, 35:309–19.

Evans, R., and Durward, L. (1984) *Maternity Rights Handbook*. Harmondsworth: Penguin Books.

Flavell, J. H., Speer, J. R., Green, F. L., and August, D. L. (1981) The development of comprehension monitoring and knowledge about communication. *Monographs of the Society for Research in Child Development*, No. 192.

Garland, C., and White, S. (1980) *Children and Day Nurseries: Management and Practice in Nine London Day Nurseries*. London: Grant McIntyre.

Garvey, C. (1979) *Play*. Cambridge, Mass.: Harvard University Press.

Gelman, R. (1979) Preschool thought. *American Psychologist*, 34:900–905.

Gelman, R., and Gallistel, C. L. (1978) *The Child's Understanding of Number*. Cambridge, Mass.: Harvard University Press.

Gesell, A. (1928) *Infancy and Human Growth*. New York: Macmillan.

Goldfarb, W. (1943) Infant rearing and problem behavior. *American Journal of Orthopsychiatry*, 13:249–65.

Goldfarb, W. (1955) Emotion and intellectual consequences of psychological deprivation in infancy: A re-evaluation. In Hoch, P. H., and Zubin, J. (eds.) *Psychopathology of Childhood*. New York: Grune and Stratton.

Goldstein, J., Freud, A., and Solnit, A. (1973) *Beyond the Interests of the Child*. New Haven: Yale University Press.

Goodman, E. (1979) *Turning Points*. New York: Random House.

Goodman, E. (1980) Observations on parenting and the women's movement. In the National Institute of Education, *Parenthood in a Changing Society*, 4–7. Urbana, Ill.: ERIC Clearinghouse on Elementary and Early Childhood Education, University of Illinois.

Hardyment, C. (1984) *Dream Babies. Child Care from Locke to Spock*. Oxford: Oxford University Press.

Harms, T., and Clifford, R. (1980) *The Early Childhood Environment Rating Scale*. New York: Teachers College Press.

Hartley, C. Gasquoine (1923) *Mother and Son*. London: Eveleigh Nash & Co.

Hartup, W. W. (1983) Peer relations. In Mussen, P. (ed.) *Handbook of Child Psychology*, 4:103–96. New York: Wiley.

Hetherington, M., Cox, M., and Cox, R. (1982) Effects of divorce on parents and children. In Lamb, M. E. (ed.) *Nontraditional Families: Parenting and Child Development*, 248–58. Hillsdale, NJ: Erlbaum.

Hoffman, L. W. (1983) *The Study of Employed Mothers over Half a Century*. Paper presented at the annual meeting of the American Psychological Association, Los Angeles, Calif.

Hostler, P. (1965) *The Child's World*. London: Benn.

Hunt, A. (1968) *Survey of Women's Employment*, Vols. 1–2, Government Social Survey. London: HMSO.

Irvine, E. E. (1952) Observations on the aims and methods of child-rearing in communal settings in Israel. *Human Relations*, 5:247–76.

James, W. (1890) *Principles of Psychology*, Vol. 1. New York: Holt, Rinehart and Winston.

Joshi, H. (1984) *Women's participation in paid work: Further analysis of the Women and Employment Survey*, Department of Employment Research Paper No. 45.

Joshi, H. (1985) Gender inequality in the labour market and the domestic division of labour. Paper for the Cambridge Journal of Economics Conference *Towards New Foundations for Socialist Britain*, Cambridge, June 1985.

Kaffman, M. A. (1965) A comparison of psychopathology: Israeli children from kibbutz and from urban surroundings. *American Journal of Orthopsychiatry*, 35:509–30.

Kagan, J. (1981) *The Second Year*. Cambridge, Mass.: Harvard University Press.

Kagan, J. (1980) Perspectives on continuity. In Brim, O. G., and Kagan, J. (eds.) *Constancy and Change in Human Development*, 26–74. Cambridge, Mass.: Harvard University Press.

Kagan, J. (1983) Classifications of the child. In Mussen, P. (ed.) *Handbook of Child Psychology*, 1:527–60. New York: Wiley.

Kagan, J., Kearsley, R., and Zelazo, P. R. (1978) *Infancy: Its Place in Human Development*. Cambridge, Mass.: Harvard University Press.

Kamerman, S. B., and Hayes, C. D. (eds.) (1982) *Families that Work: Children in a Changing World*. Washington, DC: National Academy Press.

Kardiner, A. (1954) The roads to suspicion, rage, apathy, and social disintegration. In Galdston, I. (ed.) *Beyond the Germ Theory*. New York: Health Education Council.

Karre, M., Leijon, A. G., Fors, A., Palme, O., Sandlund, M. B., and Thorsell, S. (1975) Social rights in Sweden before school starts. In Roby, P. (ed.) *Child Care – Who Cares?* 137–53. New York: Basic Books.

Kellam, S. G., Brown, C. H., Rubin, B. R., and Ensminger, M. E. (1983) Paths leading to teenage psychiatric symptoms and substance use: Developmental epidemiological studies in Woodlawn. In Guzz, S. N., Earl, F. I., and Barrett, J. W. (eds.) *Childhood Psychopathology and Development*. New York: Raven Press.

Kessen, W. (1965) *The Child*. New York: Wiley.

Klaus, M. H., and Kennell, J. H. (1976) *Maternal-Infant Bonding*. St Louis, Mo.: Mosby.

Komar, I. (1983) *Living the Dream: A Documentary Study of the Twin Oaks Community*. Norwood, Pa.: Norwood Editions.

Lamb, M. E. (1975) *The Role of the Father in Child Development*. New York: Wiley.

Lamb, M. E. (1982) Parental behavior and child development in non-traditional families: An introduction. In Lamb, M. (ed.) *Nontraditional Families: Parenting and Child Development*, 1–14. Hillsdale, NJ: Erlbaum.

Lamb, M. E., Frodi, A. M., Hwang, C. P., and Frodi, M. (1982) Varying degrees of paternal involvement in infant care: Attitudinal and behavioral correlates. In Lamb, M. (ed.) *Nontraditional Families: Parenting and Child Development*, 117–38. Hillsdale, NJ: Erlbaum.

Lasch, C. (1979) *Haven in a Heartless World: The Family Besieged*. New York: Basic Books.

Leach, P. (1986) *The First Six Months*. London: Fontana.

Lewis, J. (1984) *Women in England 1870–1950*. Sussex: Wheatsheaf.

Lipsitt, L. P. (1977) Taste in the human neonate: Its effect on sucking and heart rate. In Weiffenbach, J. M. (ed.) *Taste and Development*. Washington, DC: US Department of Health, Education, and Welfare.

Main, M., and Weston, D. R. (1981) Security of attachment to mother and father: Related to conflict behavior and readiness to establish new relationships. *Child Development*, 52:932–40.

Martin, J., and Roberts, C. (1984) *Women and Employment. A Lifetime Perspective*. London: HMSO.

Masters, J., and Wellman, H. (1974) The study of human infant attachment: A procedural critique. *Psychological Bulletin*, 81:218–37.

Mayall, B., and Petrie, P. (1983) *Childminding and Day Nurseries*. London: Heinemann.

McCartney, K., Scarr, S., Phillips, D., and Grajek, S. (1983) Day care as intervention: Comparisons of varying quality programs. Paper presented at the biennial meeting of the Society for Research in Child Development, Detroit, Mich.

McCartney, K., Scarr, S., Phillips, D., Grajek, S., and Schwarz, J. C. (1982) Environmental differences among day care centers and their effects on children's development. In Zigler, E. F., and Gordon, E. W. (eds.) *Day Care: Scientific and Social Policy Issues*, 126–51. Boston: Auburn House.

Moss, P. (1985) The proposed directive on parental leave. Paper to the Seminar on public child-care facilities and parental leave. Rome, March 1985.

Nash, J. (1956) It's time father got back into the family. Cited in Nash, J. (1976) Historical and social changes in the perception of the role of the father. In Lamb, M. (ed.) *The Role of the Father in Child Development*, 62–88. New York: Wiley.

Nash, J. (1976) Historical and social changes in the perception of the role of the father. In Lamb, M. (ed.) *The Role of the Father in Child Development*, 62–88. New York: Wiley.

National Childcare Campaign (1985) *Childcare for all: a National Childcare Campaign discussion paper*. London: National Childcare Campaign.

NCMA (1984) Topical Information Paper No. 1. London: National Childminding Association.

Newson, J., and Newson, E. (1968) *Four Years Old in an Urban Community*. London: Allen and Unwin.

Newson, J., and Newson, E. (1976) *Seven Years Old in the Home Environment*. London: Allen and Unwin.

O'Connell, J. C. (1983) Children of working mothers: What the research tells us. *Young Children: Research in Review*, 38: 63–70.

Osborn, A. F., Butler, N. R., and Morris, A. C. (1984) *The Social Life of Britain's Five-year-olds*. London: Routledge and Kegan Paul.

Parke, R. D. (1981) *Fathers*. Cambridge, Mass.: Harvard University Press.

Parke, R. D., and Sawin, D. B. (1980) The family in early infancy: Social and interactional and attitudinal analyses. In Pederson, F. A. (ed.) *The Father–infant Relationship: Observational studies in a family context*. New York: Praeger.

Pollock, L. (1983) *Forgotten Children*. Cambridge: Cambridge University Press.

Provence, S. (1982) Infant day care: Relationships between theory and practice. In Zigler, E. F., and Gordon, E. W. (eds.) *Day Care: Scientific and Social Policy Issues*, 33–55. Boston: Auburn House.

Rabin, A. I. (1965) *Growing Up in the Kibbutz*. New York: Springer.

Rabin, A. I. (1971) *Kibbutz Studies*. East Lansing, Mich.: Michigan State University Press.

Rabin, A. I., and Beit-Hallahmi, B. (1982) *Twenty Years Later: Kibbutz Children Grown Up*. New York: Springer.

Radin, N. (1982) Primary caregiving and role-sharing fathers. In Lamb, M. (ed.) *Nontraditional Families: Parenting and Child Development*, 173–204. Hillsdale, NJ: Erlbaum.

Research and Information Committee, PPA (1982) *Families in Playgroups*. London: Pre-School Playgroups Association.

Riley, D. (1983) *War in the Nursery: Theories of the Child and Mother*. London: Virago.

Roby, P. (1975) What other nations are doing. In Roby, P. (ed.) *Child Care – Who Cares?*, 133–6. New York: Basic Books.

Rothman, S. M. (1978) *Woman's Proper Place*. New York: Basic Books.

Ruopp, R. R., and Travers, J. (1982) Janus faces day care: Perspectives on quality and cost. In Zigler, E. F., and Gordon, E. W. (eds.) *Day Care: Scientific and Social Policy Issues*, 72–101. Boston: Auburn House.

Russell, G. (1982) Shared-caregiving families: An Australian study. In Lamb, M. (ed.) *Nontraditional Families: Parenting and Child Development*, 139–71. Hillsdale, NJ: Erlbaum.

Rutter, M. (1982a) Social-emotional consequences of day care for preschool children. In Zigler, E. F., and Gordon, E. W. (eds.) *Day Care: Scientific and Social Policy Issues*, 3–32. Boston: Auburn House.

Rutter, M. (1982b) *Maternal Deprivation Reassessed*. Second edition. London: Penguin.

Sagi, A. (1982) Antecedents and consequences of various degrees of paternal involvement in child rearing: The Israeli project. In Lamb, M. (ed.) *Nontraditional Families: Parenting and Child Development*, 139–71. Hillsdale, NJ: Erlbaum.

Santrock, J. W., Warshak, R. A., and Elliott, G. L. (1982) Social development and parent-child interaction in father-custody and stepmother families. In Lamb, M. (ed.) *Nontraditional Families: Parenting and Child Development*, 289–314. Hillsdale, NJ: Erlbaum.

Scarr, S. (1983) The danger of having pet variables. Paper presented at the Nags Head, North Carolina, Conference on Women, Children, and Social Policy.

Scarr, S., and McCartney, K. (1983) How people make their own environments: A theory of genotype – environment effects. *Child Development*, 54:424–35.

Scarr, S., and Weinberg, R. A. (1978) The influence of 'family background' on intellectual attainment. *American Sociological Review*, 43:674–92.

Scarr, S., and Weinberg, R. A. (1983) The Minnesota adoption studies: Malleability and genetic differences. *Child Development*, 54:260–67.

Schaffer, H. R. (1977) *Mothering*. Cambridge, Mass.: Harvard University Press.

Schaffer, H. R., and Emerson, P. (1964) The development of social attachments in infancy. *Monographs of the Society for Research in Child Development*, No. 94.

Scharlieb, M. (1912) *Womanhood and Race Regeneration*. London: Cassell.

Siegel, E., Bauman, K. E., Schaefer, E. S. (1980) Hospital and home support during infancy: impact on maternal attachment, child abuse, and neglect, and health care utilization. *Pediatrics*, 66: 183.

Sinfield, A. (1978) The social costs of unemployment. In Jones, K. *Yearbook of Social Policy in Britain 1976*. London: Routledge and Kegan Paul.

Singer, J. L., and Singer, D. G. (1982) Psychologists look at television: Cognitive, developmental, personality, and social policy implications. *American Psychologist*, 38:826–34.

Spiro, M. (1958) *Children of the Kibbutz*. Cambridge, Mass.: Harvard University Press.

Spitz, R. A. (1945) Hospitalism: An inquiry into the genesis of psychiatric conditions in early childhood. *Psychoanalytic Study of the Child*, 1:153–72.

Svejda, M., Campos, J., and Emde, R. N. (1980) Mother-infant 'bonding': Failure to generalize. *Child Development*, 51:775–9.

Swedish Institute (1984) *Childcare Programmes in Sweden.* London: Swedish Institute.

Sylva, K., Roy, C., and Painter, M. (1980) *Childwatching at Playgroup and Nursery School.* London: Grant McIntyre.

Tavris, C., and Wade, C. (1984) *The Longest War: Sex Differences in Perspective* (2nd ed.). New York: Harcourt Brace Jovanovich.

Thomas, A., and Chess, S. (1977) *Temperament and Development.* New York: Brunner/Mazel.

Tizard, B., and Hughes, M. (1984) *Young Children Learning.* London: Fontana.

Tizard, J., Moss, P., and Perry, J. (1976) *All Our Children.* London: Temple Smith.

Wachs, T. D., and Gruen, G. E. (1982) *Early Experience and Human Development.* New York: Plenum Press.

Watson, J. (1928) *Psychological Care of Infant and Child.* New York: Norton.

White, B. L. (1981) Viewpoint: Should you stay home with your baby? *Young Children,* 37:11–17.

Wolfenstein, M. (1955) Fun morality: An analysis of recent American child-training literature. In Mead, M., and Wolfenstein, M. (eds.), *Childhood in Contemporary Cultures.*

Zablocki, B. D. (1971) *The Joyful Community: An Account of the Bruderhof, a Communal Movement now in its Third Generation.* Chicago: University of Chicago Press.

Ziegler, M. E. (1983) *Assessing Parents' and Children's Time Together.* Paper presented at the annual meeting of The Society for Research in Child Development, Detroit, Mich.

Zigler, E. F. and Cascione, R. (1980) On being a parent. In National Institute of Education, *Parenthood in a Changing Society.* Urbana, Ill.: ERIC Clearinghouse on Elementary and Early Childhood Education, University of Illinois.

Zuckermann, M. (1975) Dr Spock: the confidence man. In Rosenberg, C. E. (ed.), *The Family in History.* Philadelphia: University of Pennsylvania Press.

Addresses of Some Useful Organizations

Advisory Centre for Education, 18 Victoria Park Square, London E9 9 PB (01-980 4596). Consumer advice on education.

British Association for Early Childhood Education, Montgomery Hall, Kennington Oval, London SE1 (01-582 8744). Encouragement of nursery education. Specialist advice, conferences.

Child Poverty Action Group, 1 Macklin Street, London WC2 (01-242 3225). Monitors the effects of Government policies on the welfare of disadvantaged children and parents.

Children's Legal Centre, 30 Crompton Terrace, London N1 2UN (01-359 6251). Watchdog organization for children's legal rights. Involved in immigration issues involving the separation of parents and children or carers and children.

Equal Opportunities Commission, Overseas House, Quay Street, Manchester M3 3HN. Monitors the working of the Sex Discrimination and Equal Pay Acts.

Gingerbread, 35 Wellington Street, London WC2E 7NB (01-240-0953) Local self-help groups for single parents.

Maternity Alliance, 59–61 Camden High St, London NW1 7JL (01-388 6337). Information and advice on maternity rights for working women.

National Campaign for Nursery Education, 3 St George's Terrace, Caterham-on-the-Hill, Surrey (0883 45447). Campaigns for increase in nursery education; coordinates and advises on local campaigns.

National Childbirth Trust, 9 Queensborough Terrace, London W2 3TB (01-221 3833). Nationwide advisory service on antenatal and childbirth period, breastfeeding and childcare, postnatal depression. Local branches with practical help, mother-to-mother support, parents' groups.

National Childcare Campaign, Wesley House, 70 Great Queen Street, London WC2B 5AX (01-405 5617/8).

National Childminding Association, 204–206 High Street, Bromley, Kent BR1 1PP (01-464 6164).

National Council for Civil Liberties, 21 Tabard Street, London SE1 (01-403 3888). Defence of civil liberties, includes a Rights of Women Unit.

National Council for Voluntary Child Care Organisations, 8 Wakely Street, London EC1 (01-833 3319). Coordinates funding for child care groups and dispenses grants for small and large child care projects.

National Out of School Alliance, Oxford House, Derbyshire Street, London E2 (01-739 4787). Concerned with the provision of holiday and out of school care for children, with supervision and programmes.

New Ways to Work, 347a Upper Street, London N1 0PD (01-226 4046). Information and advice on job sharing.

One Parent Families, 255 Kentish Town Road, London NW5 2LX (01-267 1361). Free confidential help on housing, law, day-care, employment.

Organisation for Parents Under Stress (also known as Parents Anonymous), 26 Manor Drive, Pickering, Yorkshire.

Pre-School Playgroups Association, Alford House, Aveline Street, London SE11 5DH (01-582 8871). Coordinates and promotes playgroup activities, training, resources and materials.

Toy Library Association, Seabrook House, Wyllotts Manor, Darkes Lane, Potters Bar, Herts EN7 2HL. Advice on how to start a toy library.

Workplace Nurseries Campaign, c/o Kingsway Children's Centre, Kingsway, London WC2 (01-242 4284).

Index